What people are saying about *UnPoverty*

Like Mark, I grew up among the poor in Africa. Both of us saw African friends suffer, and even die, from the ravages of poverty. We have much to learn from the poor, and this book affords us a glimpse into their insights.

WESS STAFFORD, PRESIDENT AND CEO, COMPASSION INTERNATIONAL

The writer of Proverbs says that one who helps the poor lends to the Lord. Mark Lutz helps show the way.

JOHN ORTBERG, AUTHOR AND SENIOR PASTOR,
MENLO PARK PRESBYTERIAN CHURCH

I grew up in South Africa, like Mark, and have seen the people he describes. He spent his life serving the poor and now shares their inspiring stories. It is an absorbing read. The stories may change your life.

PETER THORRINGTON, CHAIR, BOARD OF DIRECTORS,
OPPORTUNITY INTERNATIONAL U.S.

As an entrepreneur, I have nothin̨ for the entrepreneurs I was privileged tc na. In this insightful book, Mark has captui ...en stories, and how we can collectively transform live ....ke "unpoverty" a reality.

DR. SANDRA DAVIS, CEO, MDA LEADERSHIP CONSULTING

Mark and I share a passion for empowering the poor. We also share the love of a good story. You will be enlightened by the stories, challenged by the need, and encouraged with the results. Mark Lutz has spent his life making the world better; now it is your turn. Unpoverty really is happening—today.

KEVIN COMPTON, CO-OWNER, SAN JOSE SHARKS (NATIONAL HOCKEY LEAGUE), SILICON VALLEY SPORTS AND ENTERTAINMENT

Do you love your family and hope your children will grow up to be healthy and productive? Do you love feeling a sense of accomplishment at the end of the day? Then, believe it or not, you have something in common with the poorest of the poor. Mark Lutz tells the stories of real people striving to succeed despite the bleakest of circumstances. I can assure you that these stories will change your thinking about whether it's possible to wipe out poverty in the world—it is.

KEN BLANCHARD, CO-AUTHOR OF *THE ONE MINUTE MANAGER*® AND *LEAD LIKE JESUS*

Joining persuasive voices arguing that extreme poverty can—and therefore must—be eliminated in our lifetime, Mark Lutz, from his on-the-ground microfinance experience, offers gripping stories helping us grasp why this worthy aspiration can become reality.

ROBERT W. LANE, RETIRED CHAIRMAN, JOHN DEERE

Every person should understand poverty—what it is and isn't. Extreme poverty can be eradicated, one life at a time. Microfinance can give dignity, self-worth, and a path for the poor to better their lives forever.

WARREN STALEY, RETIRED CHAIRMAN AND CEO, CARGILL

By sharing compelling stories from some of the world's impoverished people and through his personal, honest reflection, Mark Lutz radically transforms our perspective about the gifts that make us truly wealthy.

MICHAEL J. MANTEL, PH.D., PRESIDENT AND CEO, LIVING WATER INTERNATIONAL

You'll find yourself inspired by Mark's passion and encouraged to act by his commitment and hope. I'm grateful for a voice like his which calls each of us to engage our minds and hearts to draw near to the billions in our world who live in extreme poverty.

GARY HAUGEN, PRESIDENT AND CEO, INTERNATIONAL JUSTICE MISSION

If those cool antipoverty ads starring Brad Pitt and Bono got you wanting to "make poverty history," read this book. Mark Lutz brings his readers face-to-face with hard-working, persistent, innovative poor people who, when you give them a chance, can make themselves a success and share their generosity with others. Lutz believes we can make extreme poverty obsolete. These stories render his radical vision plausible.

DAVID NEFF, EDITOR-IN-CHIEF AND VICE PRESIDENT, CHRISTIANITY TODAY MEDIA GROUP

UnPoverty challenges the developed world's common wisdom about what poverty is and who is actually poor. It sheds light on what the world's financially poor can teach us about generosity and community.

MARGO DAY, WORLD VISION MAJOR DONOR; CO-CHAIR FOR CHILD PROTECTION, WORLD VISION'S NATIONAL LEADERSHIP COUNCIL

I know the poverty that Mark Lutz describes from personal experience. This is a must-read book for all those who genuinely seek to raise themselves from the poverty that I experienced, or that they may be experiencing right now. Mark hits the nail on the head—extreme poverty can be eradicated with the right kind of empowering support.

REV. DR. KWABENA DARKO, DARKO FARMS & CO., LTD., GHANA

Having traveled extensively in developing countries with The Coca-Cola Company and, most recently, with World Vision to Africa, I see how clearly this book captures the unexpected attributes of the very poor. Mark's personal stories bring to life their amazing sense of community, gratitude, self-reliance, and ingenuity, as well as their deep, abiding faith in God and His redemptive plan. You won't want to put *UnPoverty* down!

BONNIE PRUETT WURZBACHER, SR. VICE PRESIDENT, GLOBAL CUSTOMER LEADERSHIP (RET.), THE COCA-COLA COMPANY

Mark Lutz has captured what I have seen to be true over and over again around the world. We have much to learn from the resilience, determination, and generosity of the families in these stories and countless more who are able to do so much if only given a chance.

JONATHAN T.M. RECKFORD, CEO,
HABITAT FOR HUMANITY INTERNATIONAL

Mark's stories and observations provide a very different perspective on the poor and turn conventional wisdom about who is better off upside-down. Finding grateful hearts and dignity among those facing such gut-wrenching hardships pushes us to rethink what is important. Mark's stories give hope and confidence that we can, individually and collectively, make a significant difference in the lives of the world's poor.

DICK GOCHNAUER, PRESIDENT AND CEO, UNITED STATIONERS

Mark Lutz has challenged us to team up with others to eradicate poverty. These stories of the poor have convinced us that, given a chance, the poor are ready to use their God-given talents to become self-sufficient. We want to be one of the givers that make this a reality.

DORIS AND DON MEYER, BAILLIE LUMBER CO., HAMBURG, NEW YORK

This is a book about hope. Through the stories of people he has met during his years in microfinance, Mark helps us see the poor through new eyes—as people who, though poor monetarily, are rich in resourcefulness, ingenuity, resilience, and faith. May we be challenged to act on their behalf to make "unpoverty" a reality.

JOANNA MOCKLER, FORMER CHAIR OF THE BOARD OF DIRECTORS, WORLD VISION U.S.

Having visited some 130 nations, I have been richly blessed by the poor people I've met. They really teach us a lot about ourselves and God. Read Mark Lutz's stories of incredible people.

AMBASSADOR TONY P. HALL, FORMER U.S. CONGRESSMAN
AND U.S. AMBASSADOR

Mark catches the plight of people in poverty. Through their stories, he shows that the path to "unpoverty" is possible when helping hands enable the poor to help themselves.

ROY L. ROGERS, PRIVATE INVESTOR,
FORMER MANAGING PARTNER, HAMBRECHT AND QUIST

Why we have enough food, clothing, and shelter is an accident of our birth. What are we to do about the injustice of those in real poverty versus our relative wealth? In this book we are challenged, yet encouraged. What could happen if more of us started lending a hand up to those in need?

DAVID WEEKLEY, CHAIRMAN, DAVID WEEKLEY HOMES

What does one do in response to the issues of poverty and justice for the poor? Mark Lutz has spent much of his life as part of the leadership team of Opportunity International, an organization that responds in a meaningful way to this question. This book reminds all of us how we can participate.

C. WILLIAM POLLARD, CHAIRMAN EMERITUS,
THE SERVICEMASTER COMPANY

Our family has inspected microfinance and other poverty alleviation programs on several continents. We've seen firsthand the transformation these interventions offer. Instead of arriving with the answers, Mark Lutz has watched and listened as he has traveled the world. Thank you, Mark, for sharing what you have learned.

KATHERINE AND ALAN BARNHART, BARNHART CRANE AND RIGGING

An inspiration. Mark Lutz has enlightened us through the stories of poor people who have proved how they can transform lives—their own as well as others—with a little help from the more fortunate of us. I have been privileged to meet a few of them. I recommend *UnPoverty* to all who dream of helping create a better and more equitable world.

FRED MCDOUGAL, FORMER CEO, MCDOUGAL LITTELL

Stories remain the most effective way to transfer truth from overloaded heads to under-developed hearts. By the end of *UnPoverty* I wondered how often I've traveled around the world and missed life's lessons from the very people I tried to help. Give this book to everyone you know who remains cynical of the need to engage "the least, the lost, and the left-behind"!

JOHN CROSBY, SENIOR PASTOR,
CHRIST PRESBYTERIAN CHURCH, EDINA, MINNESOTA

In this poignant book, the quiet lives of voiceless people struggling to survive on the margins speak out powerfully. Mark Lutz invites us to walk with him into the world of grinding poverty seldom seen by outsiders. *UnPoverty* is a treasure of inspiration and encouragement for those who desire to make a difference in their world.

BOB LUPTON, FOUNDER AND PRESIDENT, FCS URBAN MINISTRIES

Our world is so small. Mark's book helps us see what we all have in common and understand how we affect each other's lives. I have known Mark for more than twenty years, and through these years I have grown to love and better understand the working poor. Mark has put his heart into this book and you will grow through Mark's experiences as I have.

JOHN WEBERG, WEBERG FURNITURE STORES

Mark Lutz is the real deal—a true friend to the poor and a master storyteller. His deeply personal reflections and insightful windows into the lives of hardworking poor people around the world are inspiring. Rich stories, indeed!

SUSY CHESTON, CO-CHAIR OF THE MICROENTERPRISE COALITION

Mark Lutz uses the power of personal stories to convincingly show how extreme poverty in much of the world can be eradicated. Everyone can learn a lot for everyday life; this is a book full of inspiration, practical advice, and call to action.

GARY SCHWAMMLEIN, EXECUTIVE VICE PRESIDENT,
WILLOW CREEK ASSOCIATION INTERNATIONAL

As an expert in international development, Mark Lutz leads us on a journey beyond our nation's borders and into communities known primarily for their physical poverty. *UnPoverty* is not idealistic optimism; rather, this is a glimpse at how the ingenuity of the world's poor could lead to a world without extreme poverty.

PETER GREER, PRESIDENT, HOPE INTERNATIONAL
AND CO-AUTHOR OF *THE POOR WILL BE GLAD*

Can we envision a world where extreme poverty is replaced with dignity and simple prosperity? This book shows us how people in developing countries are undoing poverty by building thriving businesses through microfinance.

RICHARD STEARNS, PRESIDENT, WORLD VISION U.S.
AND AUTHOR OF *THE HOLE IN OUR GOSPEL*

Can we really eradicate severe poverty? Mark Lutz makes a strong case that we can. These inspiring stories give the world's poor their rightful dignity and showcase their determination to earn their way out of poverty.

BOB BUFORD, FOUNDER, LEADERSHIP NETWORK,
AND AUTHOR OF *HALFTIME* AND *FINISHING WELL*

Our abundance can render us tone-deaf to the needs of the extremely poor, yet we have more in common with them than we may realize. We value hard work. We care about each other. We act in good faith. We are proud of ourselves when we make a difference. Mark Lutz shows us how.

CLAUDIA KENNEDY, RETIRED LIEUTENANT GENERAL, U.S. ARMY

Two thousand Bible verses call on us to respond to the needs of the poor. Eliminating poverty can be accomplished through job creation. Mark Lutz tells amazing stories of how that happens. These microenterprises clearly demonstrate that economic improvement comes from the bottom up.

TONY CAMPOLO, PROFESSOR EMERITUS, EASTERN UNIVERSITY

This book is redemptive and an inspiration. Mark's deep analysis will be a great encouragement to third-world readers and a transformational instruction to the western world. He encourages us to respect, trust, and facilitate this positive change. Poverty anywhere in this world can be eradicated. I hope many will be joining the growing chorus that "it can be done!"

THE RT. REV. JOHN RUCYAHANA, BISHOP OF SHYIRA DIOCESE, RWANDA

UnPoverty

UnPoverty

*Rich Lessons
from the Working Poor*

MARK LUTZ

*Foreword by Rich Stearns,
President of World Vision U.S.*

UnPoverty Communications

Glen Ellyn, Illinois

For further information about *UnPoverty*, contact:
UnPoverty Communications
P.O. Box 3112
Glen Ellyn, IL 60138
mark@unpoverty.org
www.unpoverty.org

For further information about World Vision, contact:
Mark Lutz, c/o World Vision
P.O. Box 9716
Federal Way, WA 98063-9716
mlutz@worldvision.org
www.worldvision.org

At the author's request, all proceeds from the sale of this book will be directed to established humanitarian organizations to help people lift themselves out of poverty.

First Edition: September 2010
Revised Edition: October 2012 (including foreword, afterword, photo insert)
Library of Congress Control Number: 2012948475
ISBN-13 978-0-9829089-2-1 hardback
ISBN-13 978-0-9829089-3-8 paperback

Publisher's Note: Stories told in this book are true, but the names of some individuals have been changed to protect their privacy.

Printed in the United States of America
2 3 4 5 6 7 8 9

To Lise

my pearl

CONTENTS

Foreword 17

Acknowledgments 19

Introduction 21

1   JUSTICE 27
    Justice is possible only when everyone has a realistic
    opportunity to meet their basic human needs.

2   FAMILY 45
    Healthy families, regardless of poverty, cultivate dignity
    and become the foundation of society.

3   COMMUNITY 63
    People in the developing world wholly embrace, participate in,
    and are enriched by community.

4   GRATITUDE 75
    True gratitude results in generosity.

5   PERSISTENCE 89
    Hardship creates persistence in a way that luxury does not.

6   SELF-RELIANCE 101
    The working poor long to break free from the chains of
    poverty and become fully self-reliant.

7   FAITH 111
    When there are no safety nets, faith takes on new meaning.

8   INNOCENCE 125
    Childhood is a luxury we must fight to protect.

9   INGENUITY 137
    The poorest entrepreneurs redefine creativity and innovation.

10 AWARENESS 149
    Thanks to technology, the whole world is watching.

11 FINAL LESSONS 165
    God loves the poor, and so should we.

Afterword 175

FOREWORD

I'm deeply thankful for people like Mark Lutz who see ending extreme global poverty not as a noble idea, but as a mission that we can't ignore. It's a mission that is worth devoting our lives to, as Mark has.

Since joining World Vision U.S. in 1998, I've visited dozens of developing countries and met countless children and families whose memories are ingrained in my heart and mind. Time and again, I've seen overwhelming poverty that keeps families from experiencing life in all its fullness. But in turn, I've observed the incredible dignity, resilience, and determination of the poor, and how—when given opportunities and support—they begin to thrive.

Mark knows this too. It's one of the many reasons we asked him to join the World Vision team in 2012 as our Director of Global Philanthropy. Mark recognizes the God-given dignity and potential inherent in each person he meets in impoverished communities around the world. Throughout the pages of *UnPoverty*, you'll see his wholehearted commitment to respecting that dignity by enabling these remarkable people to change their own circumstances.

Extending opportunities to these entrepreneurs is an absolutely critical component of successful development work. By equipping the hardworking poor with capital to start businesses, we empower them to create their own solutions, foster community development, and lay an essential foundation for abundant life. This makes all the other work that organizations like World Vision do sustainable—efforts like drilling wells, helping families grow nutritious food, and providing access to education.

Like Mark, I believe it's possible to end extreme poverty. As you'll see for yourself in the following pages, the poor are able, willing, and eager to create a better future for themselves and their children. Many of them have brilliant ideas that could change their families, their communities, and just possibly the world.

The good news is that we can make their ideas achievable.

In *UnPoverty*, Mark not only tells the stories of the poor, he also lays out the steps for us to join him in responding to their need. It's surprisingly simple, as you'll discover for yourself. You'll also be happy to know that the proceeds from your purchase of this book will be used to help people lift themselves out of poverty.

I hope you will be encouraged and inspired to join the growing army of passionate people working together to help build a world in which extreme poverty is undone—for good.

Rich Stearns
President, World Vision U.S.
Author, *The Hole in Our Gospel*

ACKNOWLEDGMENTS

Telling stories is easy when they are about heroic people. Countless poor people around the world make this storytelling possible. They are the heroes of this book, though they'll never know it.

I have been honored to meet them. Their richness overwhelms me and I'm proud to speak on their behalf. Brothers and sisters around the world and esteemed members of our global village, thank you for your inspiration.

Writing a book, however, especially one about many different unrelated people, is different from storytelling. Taking all those tales and weaving facts and feelings together into one written document, required the eyes—and ruthless scissors—of a seasoned writer. I'm thankful for the experience and sensitivity of Lyn Cryderman, who has served as my editorial consultant.

One person without whom this book would have remained a dream for another year is Edythe Draper. She has served as coach, mentor, cheerleader—and needed slave driver—from the time we met. Asking for nothing in return, she brought to bear her years of experience as writer, editor, and project manager, somehow keeping its myriad plates spinning. Edie, on behalf of poor people all over the world whose lives will be transformed as a result, but who will never get to meet you, I thank you. And Martha Haley, I'm indebted to you for introducing me to Edie.

This final product is the apex of a journey that started more than a decade ago. One person walked with me every step, including down rabbit trails and across a desert. Lise, no one, including you, will ever know how much you have influenced this project. Your patience in reading and reacting to the same chapter one more time; your candid yet loving critique even when you knew I didn't want to make more changes; our travel together in Colombia, South Africa, and Zimbabwe, especially your tender connection with Esther; your keen awareness of international events and issues that protected me from more than a few landmines; your encouragement to make this my voice and passion; and your belief that it could become a reality—for all this and so much more, thank you.

One of the most enjoyable and unexpected dimensions to this project has been the active participation of my family, particularly toward the end. Nate, you nailed it with the title. Bravo. Andrea and Hollie, thanks for your support, prayers, feedback on cover and content, and for what you've offered to do to fuel this flame. And Josh, what can I say about your music? You are one talented songwriter. I can't wait for readers to hear you sing about the people and tales from these pages. Mom, it has been great sharing my struggles and ideas with a veteran author. I'm so proud of you and thank you for our shared love.

Thank you, board members and staff at Opportunity International— my family for more than twenty-two years—for encouraging me to tell these stories of people we all respect and admire. Finally: thank you, John Clause and World Vision, for embracing the idea to reprint this book and continue its impact for the sake of the poor. Thanks to everyone in Creative Solutions who helped me with both the minor and not-so-minor tweaks as we made revisions for this second printing. And a special thanks to Jon Warren for the amazing photographs that complement the ideas and stories presented in this book. May both Opportunity International and World Vision prosper as we seek to offer hope and dignity to the poorest members of our global village—the heroes of *UnPoverty*.

INTRODUCTION

unpoverty   [uhn-**pov**-er-tee]—**noun**

1. the state of eradicating extreme poverty
2. the reversal of a perpetual state of deprivation
3. the provision of basic human needs
Base word origin: 1175; Medieval English *poverte* <
Old French poverte < Latin *paupertatem*, small means

Much of what we learn and read about the poor has kept them distant and impersonal. They have become an intellectual category, a problem to be solved. Some politicians and policymakers may find that useful, but if we want to achieve unpoverty, we need to know these people as unique and worthy human beings. A mother living on the streets of Kolkata loves her child as much as a mother living in a gated community in suburban Chicago. A child helping his father scavenge through garbage has the same right to an education as a youngster enjoying recess on her school playground in Orange County.

I hope that by coming with me into the homes and daily lives of some of the poorest of the poor, you will see them with new eyes. Rather than pity them for their poverty, I hope you will respect them, learn from them, and maybe even recognize yourself in their hopes, dreams, and spirits. Just like you, the poor want to enjoy their families, prosper, and reach out to help someone else. That is the way I believe that extreme poverty will become obsolete.

For twenty-five years I've visited the cardboard and tarpaper huts of families who live on garbage dumps. I've hiked dusty paths to African villages whose names do not appear on most maps. I've tiptoed across makeshift bridges over open sewers that give new meaning to the term "waterfront homes."

For most of that time, the purpose of my travel was business, but I didn't wear a power suit or negotiate multimillion-dollar contracts in richly paneled board rooms or over sumptuous meals in elegant restaurants. The clients I worked with were not vice presidents or CEOs, and you will not find their businesses on the Fortune 500 list.

Yet.

You see, for more than two decades I worked for an organization that provides small loans to very poor people in the developing world so they can start businesses and feed their families. The technical term is *microenterprise development* or *microfinance*. Whereas a start-up business in the United States might seek several million dollars in venture capital, the typical initial microloan is less than $150. These are not gifts, but real loans with interest and payment schedules. Before prospective business owners receive their loan, they are required to develop business plans that must be approved by a loan officer. By just about any conventional standard, these clients would not qualify as even high-risk borrowers. Credit checks are out of the question because they live in a barter- and cash-only world. Many microloans are made to people who don't officially exist because they have no identification papers, no passports, and no birth certificates.

Most of the businesses I worked with were tiny in revenue, but giants in resourcefulness, innovation, and entrepreneurship. When it comes to supply-chain management, containing labor costs, liquidity, return on investment, and net profit margin, these businesses could teach Fortune 500 companies a few things. And while I know many fine business leaders in the West who are tireless workers, no one outworks the business owners I have met in the developing world.

You would think that loaning money to people so poor might create a huge number of defaults, but the overall record of microfinance institutions is very good. Of the more than one million loans my organization made each year, only two to five percent defaulted. Something tells me that most banks in the United States would love that kind of record.

When I began working in international development, I held the common view that while we need to reach out and help the poor as much as possible, we will never eliminate poverty. Isn't it just a fact of life?

Much of what was then called the "third world," particularly Africa, was considered hopeless. Massive aid from developed nations had poured into those regions with little or no overall improvement. And the attitude among many ordinary citizens in the United States was that we had too many problems in our own country to be concerned about remote villages around the world. As a follower of Jesus, I accepted the faulty interpretation of the Bible that "the poor you will always have with you." Still, I was committed to doing my part to try to make a difference. Like most people, I did not believe we could eliminate poverty, at least not in my lifetime. Now, after more than two decades of working closely with some of the poorest people living in some of the poorest nations, I've changed my mind.

About 1.3 billion people today survive on $1.25 a day. These people are not the problem. Rather, they are assets. They remain mired in poverty primarily because of latitude and longitude, not laziness or stupidity. Every day's work earns that day's meal, with nothing left over to build on, and no hope of escape. With strategic empowerment from others, however, these survivors prove they can be a large part of the solution.

I believe we can eradicate extreme poverty. And if we can, then we must. I'm not alone. Today an encouraging wind of change is moving us away from the previous notion that the poor are an inevitable presence, siphoning off crumbs of what the wealthy produce. Fueled by the voices and actions of prominent leaders, many are no longer conceding that more than a billion people must endure life in absolute poverty. I see a growing desire to cause radical change that will force our grandchildren to learn about extreme poverty in history books. Events such as the U.N. Millennium Summit in 2000, Muhammad Yunus winning the 2006 Nobel Peace Prize, and authors like Jeffrey Sachs writing about it have convinced many of us that we will see an end to extreme poverty during our lifetime. Bill Gates, Warren Buffett, Pierre Omidyar, and other philanthropists have made strategic international charity cool, rendering social entrepreneurship the vogue. Entertainers like Bono have popularized social justice. Oprah skyrocketed the early growth of Kiva, another microfinance organization. Clearly, the idea that extreme poverty can be eradicated has reached the tipping point.

It hasn't hurt that we are more connected to people around the world than ever before, reminding us that we are part of a global community and that as such, we cannot be concerned about only our own welfare. The Internet, email, social networks, cell phones, and 24/7 international news channels bring the *favelas* of Brazil and the slums of Manila into our living rooms. Even our entertainment invites us to consider both the dignity and destitution of the poor and oppressed. Who can forget the harshness of child slavery in "Slumdog Millionaire"? Globalization has made us more aware that the majority of our extended family members are desperately poor.

As awareness expands, our attitudes evolve. Simply because some members have a different complexion, live ten thousand miles away in strikingly different cultures, and have minimal education, they are no less valuable or deserving. Though there have been many well-intentioned yet faulty attempts to help the poor in the past, a new spirit is emerging, one that says, "Convince me that a solution is significant, sustainable, and scalable—and I'm on board."

That's what I hope to do in this book—instill in you a spirit of optimism and hope about poor people. I will show you that unpoverty is possible; that we can undo extreme poverty. I will demonstrate this remarkable claim by telling you true stories of the working poor who needed only a bootstrap opportunity to help themselves. Given that opportunity, they are undoing the chains of poverty and providing opportunities to others in their communities. What I have learned most from the poor is that they are poor only in material terms. Their poverty doesn't define their character or their desire to better themselves and their families.

That's the second thing I hope to show you in this book—a new understanding and appreciation for the poor.

Finally, by the time you finish reading it, I hope you will see why I consider it a privilege to work with people whose financial net worth is often less than the value of my wristwatch. Like many who work in international development, I went into this career sincerely hoping to help the poor by helping them help themselves. Although it is gratifying to see that this really does work, the poor have taught me far more than I could ever teach them. As a white, fairly well-educated, affluent

Christian American, I thought I knew all about things like family and faith and gratitude. From the poor, I have learned that so much of what I thought I knew only scratched the surface. They have given me a deeper understanding of the things that really matter in life. For that I am grateful.

So while this book is primarily about desperately poor yet abundantly rich and generous individuals, it is also about my own personal journey. Some of the profound moments and pivotal junctures of my life have occurred in the developing world. When I'm with the poorest of the poor, I somehow feel closer to God. I feel connected and energized. There have been times I have wept uncontrollably when confronted and confounded by nearly unbearable privation. Yet those encounters have caused me to acknowledge that I am the one most bankrupt. As I begin to appreciate their wealth, I start to recognize my own contrasting hunger and nakedness.

Do I really believe we can undo extreme poverty—people living on $1.25 a day—in my lifetime? Given the fact that I am already middle-aged, that's an ambitious goal, but yes, I really do believe it.

My desire is that these stories will help you better understand the riches of the poor, affirming their intrinsic value, so that you will join the economic revolution to find ways to support and empower them.

I know we can create a world of unpoverty, and it will happen a lot faster if we have one more important resource.

You.

1

JUSTICE

Justice is possible only when everyone has a

realistic opportunity to meet their basic human needs.

My journey to the Taj Mahal begins with a two-mile cab ride that ends a mile short of that stunning monument. The Indian government has banned motorized vehicles beyond this point to protect this white marble "jewel of Muslim art" from the defacing smog. Elaborately decorated rickshaws transport streams of tourists from the designated boundary to our final destination. Our transport is a standard black bicycle with a frame someone lengthened by a couple of feet, a bicycle "stretch limo." It has a padded vinyl rear seat rising high above the operator's shoulders. This single-gear vehicle weighs well over a hundred pounds and includes a retractable canopy that shields passengers while leaving the operator exposed to the elements. Painted bright yellow and crimson and dotted with garish illustrations, this common mode of transportation looks intrinsically connected to the colorful, urban Indian landscape.

Achir, my interpreter, and I board the exotic machine, eager to experience the Taj Mahal at sunrise. Through Achir, I talk to the driver during our fifteen-minute ride to the entrance gate. Determined to earn enough money to feed his family for the day, he had been waiting almost an hour at the depot for a passenger. At five o'clock, I am his first customer. He hopes he will make about $10 by the time the Taj closes at sunset.

Like me, he has three children. Our similarities end there. His family belongs to the layer of people living near the base of the world's financial pyramid, where nearly three billion humans exist on about $2 per day. He works seven days a week. If he misses a day, his family doesn't eat that day. He doesn't own the rickshaw, but leases it at usurious rates, thus forfeiting much of the profit that would eventually enable him to purchase it. Even though he is industrious and hardworking, the never-ending grind of poverty holds him fast.

Hundreds of thousands of Indian men are doomed from birth by their families' caste to pursue this brutal vocation. Born on this eternal treadmill, they have no alternatives, they make no progress, and they have next to no hope of ever getting off.

When we approach the Taj Mahal, the early morning air is thick and humid. Our driver sweats profusely and I wonder what it will be like for him as the sun climbs overhead. Why am I perched comfortably here at the back of the rickshaw while he pedals me along? I wonder about other things. Does he deserve his life of drudgery while I enjoy mine of luxury? It is not an easy question to answer, and what happens next is even more unsettling.

I reach into my pocket to pay him, but he raises his hand, saying something to my translator, who explains. "He would rather wait to take you back, and then you can pay him."

I look briefly at the operator and then respond to Achir, "But I'll be a while and he could collect another fare from someone else."

My native companion interprets the words as well as the cultural context: "Yes, but work is scarce, you see. At least if he waits, he knows he has another job."

The Mughal emperor Shah Jahan created the Taj Mahal—often called the eighth wonder of the world—out of deep devotion to his wife, whom he passionately loved through their eighteen years together. She died in 1631 while giving birth to their fourteenth child. After her death, construction on the majestic monument began and continued every day for the next twenty-two years, employing twenty thousand workers. Shah Jahan erected the memorial on a raised marble platform 186 feet by 186 feet. A central dome is of equal height. Ten thousand elephants transported stone many miles.

I am arriving at dawn to bask in the beauty of the Taj Mahal, looking on as the sun rises over the matchless shrine. Although the tranquil mausoleum today stands near a murky cesspool, the Taj Mahal itself lives up to its reputation. As the sun comes up, thousands of hand-cut and meticulously inlaid semiprecious stones gradually appear like stars in the night sky, responding to the changing light. I stand in awe as the sun's rays illuminate first the eastern edge of this wonder, then gracefully dance westward, casting shadows as only sunlight can at this time of day. Within an hour, the entire edifice glistens. Colors spring to life. Pristine marble that glows pink at night dons again its brilliant white.

When I return to the entrance, I find the rickshaw operator chatting patiently with one of the dozens of other drivers. After a brief word with my interpreter, I learn of a new wrinkle.

"He says he can return us to your hotel, rather than merely back to the depot," Achir explains.

"Does he know how far that is?" I wonder out loud. "We're talking three miles!"

Another exchange between Achir and the driver. Obviously the rickshaw driver is aware of the distance, and is pleased. He shakes his head strongly from side to side, the Indian equivalent of our Western affirmative, up-and-down nod.

Not in any rush, I agree and we set off. Still only mid-morning, the air is noticeably hotter. Dense traffic congests the narrow streets. In no time, beads of sweat on the operator's neck drip down his back. We pass beggars too maimed to walk, scavengers sorting through last night's garbage in hopes of finding something to eat or sell, street vendors carrying their entire inventory in overloaded hands, and an unending swarm of bicycle and rickshaw riders, all trying to earn enough money to buy a handful of rice before the end of the day.

I have visited India twice before and I am aware of how the economy is growing, but the intense poverty shocks me anew. I am jarred even more this time by the hordes of poor people. Crushing throngs move everywhere.

Coming to a slight incline, we gradually slow down despite the driver standing on the pedals with all his weight. His is no mountain bike with fifteen gears like the one I use for pleasure. Our rickshaw operator is strong, but his single-geared bicycle is no match for our combined 350 pounds and the small hill. We grind to a halt. Without any hesitation, he steps to the ground, leans firmly into the handlebars, and with one slow step after another, he pushes us up the hill. Why that humble act penetrates so deeply I do not fully understand, but I find myself in tears. The short distance between my cushioned seat and his immobile pedals sets up an epiphany. I see in that moment the huge, unjust gap between the rich and the poor.

What is justice in this age of globalization? What does kindness look like in today's interconnected place called Earth? More than two thousand years ago, a Hebrew prophet proposed a similar challenge, asking a rhetorical question that he quickly went on to answer about the meaning of life. What does our Creator expect of us? Must we sacrifice our firstborn child to please God? Absolutely not! Micah distills all of life down to one simple, all-encompassing query about what the Creator wants from those he created:

> He has told you, O man, what is good;
> and what does the LORD require of you
> but to do justice, and to love kindness,
> and to walk humbly with your God?
> –Micah 6:8 (ESV)

At the end of my ride, I smile and hand the rickshaw operator $2.50, about a fourth of what he hopes to earn during the entire day. He holds out his hand asking for more. It would be just as easy to give him $25 or even $250. I feel I should pay more, and to this day I am mortified that I did not. Instead I obeyed my translator who insisted I not give the driver any more. Wouldn't a tip of $20 have tipped the scales of justice in the right direction? What should I have done based on Jesus' mission articulated in the synagogue as he read from the Hebrew prophet Isaiah? "'The Spirit of the Lord is on me, because he has anointed me to preach good news to the poor. He has sent me to proclaim freedom for the prisoners and recovery of sight for the blind, to release the oppressed'" (Luke 4:18).

Seeking to follow the example Jesus set, how do I bring good news to the poor and free the oppressed? How do I do justice this day in India or next week in Chicago?

INJUSTICE UP CLOSE AND PERSONAL

Even as a child, I could not escape questions of justice. From the time I was a one-year-old until I returned to the United States in 1970 to attend college, I lived with my missionary parents in South Africa, under a political system where 75 percent of the population was classified non-white, allowing only a fraction of them to reach economic prosperity. My mother and father worked every day in Soweto, the acronym for the "southwest township" where blacks who labored in Johannesburg were forced to live. Apartheid law required my parents to return to our all-white community every night. Given a choice, we would have lived among those my parents came to serve, but injustice ultimately restricts everyone.

Without breaking the strict laws enforcing apartheid, which would have resulted in deportation, my parents bent as many rules as they dared. To our white neighbors' disdain, we regularly held gatherings and served meals in our home for black people who had never entered a white person's house as a guest. Yet even though we welcomed them into our home, they were still inhibited by the all-pervasive atmosphere and rules of apartheid. On one occasion, my father happened upon a black guest urinating in our garden because he did not believe white people would allow a black man to use their bathroom.

During the summer of 2003, after twenty-five years of marriage, my wife and I visited my roots in Johannesburg. That was Lise's debut in Africa. With the apartheid system abolished nine years previously, much had changed since my childhood. We drove to the suburb where I grew up, on the outskirts of what was then an eight-mile buffer zone separating whites from Soweto.

I showed her our house, which seemed to have shrunk to half the size of my childhood recollection. I pointed out the detached servants' quarters at the back of each house, since even blue-collar families could afford a full-time maid. I noted how the drab, unkempt yards of today contrasted with yesterday's lawns and gardens, immaculately manicured by black gardeners and "houseboys."

We visited my public high school, reserved for white children, approximately twenty-five to a class. The black children attended government schools in Soweto, where the class size would be three times as large, the rooms unheated, teachers poorly paid and educated, books inferior if available at all, and almost no money spent on athletics and other afterschool activities. Virtually no university education was available for the non-white population in the country—three out of four people. Very few families managed to scrape together and sacrifice enough to pay school fees and buy books so that even one of their children could continue past the tenth grade. Only one in ten of the smattering who eventually did make it to the end passed the final matriculation exam. The exam, required for graduation, written and graded by the all-white establishment, was identical for all ethnic groups: Afrikaans, English, Black, Colored, and Indian. This insidious tactic, instigated by the ruling white government, ensured that non-whites would never become educated and threaten white control.

I took Lise down the path where I remember riding my bicycle with my high school friends. One good friend in particular would make sport of riding past black pedestrians, reaching out his hand and knocking the hats off the heads of elderly men, shouting, "Watch out, *kaffir!*" It was the ultimate derogatory insult, our version of the N-word.

From infancy this young man had been indoctrinated to believe that blacks were mentally handicapped, culturally destitute, and morally bankrupt. White children accepted the propaganda from their parents, teachers, and religious leaders, believing they were genetically superior in every way to blacks. It is difficult to understand how, for more than forty years, good and God-fearing people perpetuated so unjust a system. How could they, from the Bible and the teachings of a loving Jesus, have defended segregation and inequality? Black children grew up with diminished dignity and self-confidence as a result of that same incessant brainwashing.

LONG-TERM EFFECT OF INJUSTICE

On this trip I witnessed how the wounds and scars from half a century of extreme injustice in South Africa do not quickly heal. Although Nelson Mandela heroically prevented a bloodbath when the all-white government and apartheid system dissolved, severe repercussions still persist. Violence and fear among all races are as common in South Africa now as were "whites only" signs and enforced segregation previously. Injustice does not condone crime, but it does help explain it. With South Africa's economy in shambles, its violent crime rate is among the highest anywhere, and it is arguably the rape capital of the world.

We visited several of the people I grew up with, including a friend whose seventeen-year-old daughter had been raped at gunpoint in her own bed—just two weeks before our visit—while he and his wife slept across the hall. He explained how the offenders poisoned and killed the watchdog, scaled the six-foot concrete fence, disengaged the alarm system, and circumvented the multiple heavy locks on the doors. When we arrived at their house, workers were busy adding barbed wire and an electric-current protection on top of the wall surrounding their property. They also installed a panic button in each room that, when triggered, alerts a security company.

Later that week, we shared a lovely dinner party with another old friend I used to play with as a child. He had taken a further step after their last burglary. In addition to steel bars over all the bedroom windows, he had recently installed a floor-to-ceiling wrought iron gate in the hallway leading from the living room to the bedrooms. Each night after everyone is in bed, they padlock the gate so that when the house is broken into again, the criminals will not be able to harm the family.

As a result of their childhood indoctrination, these friends of mine may not have recognized how they were oppressing black people during apartheid. Obviously, many scars that were inflicted then still fester.

Often the privileged class justifies their treatment of the poor by saying they are lazy or ignorant or angry and need to be controlled. Having visited some fifty countries, many of them in the developing world, I have become increasingly convinced that the majority of the world's poorest people are poor through no fault of their own. Extreme poverty is not caused by laziness, but by latitude and longitude. Most of the world's poor are decent, hardworking people who have been victimized by unjust systems that erect insurmountable hurdles wherever they turn. Corrupt governments with untenable national debts control their lives. They have no legal property rights and consequently no collateral. Ancient cultural traditions place overwhelming restrictions on women. There are trade barriers, and no access to credit, insurance, safe banking, or a legal system. To add insult to injury, many of the poorest people in the world live in regions with either too little or too much rainfall, infertile soil, and other geographic conditions that make survival a daily struggle.

These climate conditions are not unjust. For example, drought itself is a natural disaster, not injustice. But drought for a family dependent on a tiny plot of maize, compared to drought in America's Midwest where there are endless acres of corn, is a very different disaster. Poverty exists in the U.S., and malnourished children do live here; but the vast majority of Americans have plentiful access to food regardless of the weather. Did I deserve to live in the Midwest where I could purchase any kind of food any time of the year? Does the father in Sudan deserve to live where life is so fragile that one bad season could result in the deaths of his children?

We can't change weather patterns or geography, but we can do something about injustice.

WHAT IS JUSTICE?

Economists, ethicists, and philosophers have written extensively about justice, but what I have learned from the working poor is that justice simply means that everyone has a realistic opportunity to meet their basic human needs. An African woman named Esther exemplifies what can happen when a person is finally given that chance.

Zimbabwe (once Rhodesia, renamed after gaining independence from an oppressive white regime in 1980) has suffered under the corrupt and unjust leadership of its strongman, President Robert Mugabe. During his thirty-year reign this once prosperous nation and breadbasket of southern Africa has become an economic wasteland, now recognized by the United Nations as the fastest-shrinking economy in the world.

Today few foreigners dare to visit Zimbabwe as it hemorrhages under immeasurable hyperinflation and strict military control. When Lise and I visited in 2003, the U.S. State Department had issued a warning against travel to Zimbabwe. Coupled with severe shortages of food and gasoline, this warning caused tourism to join the rhinoceros on the list of endangered species. The shrinking economy rewarded my wife and me with a bus entirely to ourselves for the two-hour journey from Victoria Falls to Hwange Game Reserve. The week we spent in Zimbabwe offered a crash course in injustice and the plight of the poor. I do not mean to suggest that the poor are less responsible for their actions; rather, to a great extent, wealth and poverty are byproducts of where we are born.

In the capital city of Harare it was shocking to drive at rush hour on roads clogged not by cars but by waves of pedestrians. With the soaring price of fuel, more and more people were unable to pay the ever-mounting cost of public transportation, which for many commuters already consumed half of their inadequate salaries. Those who lived too far to walk were forced to quit their jobs. For an increasing number of regular citizens, the solution was to migrate from the big cities to rural areas, where at least they could plant vegetables and feed their families.

The global HIV and AIDS pandemic, which has killed thirty million people and infected another thirty-four million worldwide, conspires alongside corruption and extreme poverty in southern African countries like Zimbabwe. Globally, more than two-thirds of all people with the disease live in sub-Saharan Africa, and the region around Zimbabwe is the pandemic's epicenter. Though Zimbabwe's HIV prevalence rate is now an estimated 13 percent, less than four years ago nearly one in four Zimbabweans were infected with the disease. Home to less than thirteen million people, Zimbabwe still sees more than twelve hundred AIDS-related deaths every week, many of them the economically active.

As life expectancy shrank to the low thirties, the government responded by increasing publicity about the symptoms of the disease and how it is spread. They also introduced a program to benefit the children of HIV-infected citizens. The program requires that people be tested, an action that in itself increases awareness and promotes behavior change. Parents with a certificate verifying their HIV-positive status are guaranteed that their children will receive free schooling after being orphaned. Today, at around fifty-two years, Zimbabwe's life expectancy is the eighth-lowest in the world—a slight improvement over several years ago, when it was tied with Afghanistan for dead last.

ESTHER'S CASH COW

We traveled to Vasho Ghon, a tiny village that does not appear on most maps. Quaintly nestled in picturesque hills three hours from Harare, this remote farming community has been home to the Shona tribe for many generations. Their ancient ancestors would feel at home here today. With no electricity or running water, many conditions have remained unchanged for hundreds of years. The most notable developments include a school for the children and the calamity of AIDS.

Individual homesteads, encased by brush and thorn bushes, dot the slopes of rolling, grass-covered hills. Each clearing offers a home to one family, with a round mud building for the man and a similar dwelling for each of his wives and their children. Vast open fields for grazing separate the enclaves, which are connected by dusty footpaths. The shallow river that gracefully meanders between the lowest points in the valley serves the drinking, cooking, washing, and irrigation needs of those living in Vasho Ghon. It was in this remote African village that I met the woman who has inspired me these many years, although our paths crossed only briefly.

Esther meets me at a narrow stream bridged with strategically placed stepping stones. Beside the water she welcomes me with a smile. Cautiously I follow as she leads me confidently across the slippery rocks. She is stylishly dressed in a two-piece suit and wearing pumps that inhibit neither her dancing nor her walking through her fields. As we walk up the hill to her home, she points out the gravestone of her husband who died four years ago, just months after their third child was born. When I try to express condolences she nonchalantly comments, "Life is difficult for mothers in my village."

Her husband had been sick for a long time. Fear kept the family from giving the symptoms a name—fear of knowing, fear of dying, fear of being stigmatized. But when Esther tested HIV-positive, she knew that the same unforgiving virus would eventually kill her. What she does not know is how much time remains for her to prepare her farm and her three young children to tend it on their own.

Much like other homesteads in the community, Esther's enjoys a few improvements. Although the basic structures are still made of roughly felled trees and are roofed with thatched grass, her husband had plastered some of the mud walls with cement before he died. He had also poured a thin layer of concrete over several of the compacted cow-dung floors. There are still no windows, but a solid wooden door, which she secures with a lock and key, hangs on steel hinges.

About half the size of a football field, Esther's compound perches on the side of a gently sloping hill that her family cleared and carefully maintains. She protects it with a barricade constructed from sticks and interlocking brambles. She sweeps the hardened, reddish dirt clean with a broom made from tree branches. Within the fenced area, two dogs, perhaps a dozen chickens, and a gaggle of six geese roam freely. Corn that Esther harvested earlier in the year is stored outside in a large bin, several feet above the ground, well out of reach of animals. The shaded area below the corn serves as home for seventy-eight chicks, which she breeds for both consumption and commerce.

The external structure may look primitive, but once inside I am impressed by how thoughtfully and tastefully she has furnished it. The single large, round chamber serves as living room and sleeping quarters for Esther and her three children. A stuffed sofa and two matching chairs grace the room, each covered with little hand-stitched hearts. On one side rests a double bed with an attractive spread and pillows. It is obvious she takes great pride in this immaculate home, ringed with handcrafted cabinets.

Adjacent to it stands another round structure, now inhabited by her sister, also widowed by some unknown, or at least unacknowledged, disease. She, too, mothered children, and she, too, tested positive for HIV. Nearby, a separate building functions as the kitchen, where the two sisters cook and feed their children.

Esther is particularly eager to show us one special building. "I built it myself," she says proudly as we cross the lot to the far corner. The smaller hut blends in with the others. It is made of mud with a thatched roof. As she opens the wooden door, with arms stretched wide, Esther gestures with glee to the sparkling white commode, the kind you'd find at Home Depot. "I bought it in Harare!" she exclaims with confidence. "And I even put in a septic tank!" Without running water, the toilet's tank must be filled by hand. "It's a good place to dump the dirty wash water."

I can picture her bringing this white porcelain fixture home, strapped on the roof of a crowded bus, along with mounds of other passengers' luggage, including perhaps a couple of live goats. How this single woman maneuvered the toilet from the spot where the dirt road ends, across the bridgeless river, and up the hill on the other side to her home, I can only imagine.

Granted, Esther and her sister have ample experience navigating that hill with heavy loads. Each morning starting at five o'clock, they begin a daily routine of trekking down the hill to the creek. With five-gallon containers balanced on their heads and one in each hand, the two women haul water to irrigate their small vegetable garden. Over the next three or four hours, they each make about twenty-five grueling trips up and down, following the well-worn footpath connecting their source of water and their source of livelihood.

Potatoes, tomatoes, and a few other vegetables provide food for their table. Most of the carefully tended raised-bed gardens, however, are dedicated to producing covo, a leafy dark green vegetable that Esther sells in the market along with her chickens and eggs.

How has this radiant woman become so self-sufficient? What motivates her to press on despite her deadly illness is something that gradually becomes clearer as we spend several hours together.

With increased publicity and information about AIDS, a couple of years ago Esther suspected she might be infected. Because her children would receive modest government assistance if she were infected, she agreed to be tested. Now she must live with the haunting memory of her husband's slow and painful death, and the near certainty that she faces a similar one. But with certification that she is HIV-positive, her children will remain in school after she dies.

Making provision for their school fees is only one component of this determined woman's aggressive plan to create self-sufficiency for her family. Daily she prepares for the inevitable, hoping and praying for their sake that it will be later rather than sooner.

For all practical purposes, unemployment in her immediate community is 100 percent. Factories, formal businesses, and regular paying jobs do not exist. Life for Esther looked hopeless. Simple farming was all she knew, and years of caring for her dying husband left the family garden and their only source of livelihood in disarray. She dreamed of owning a cow so she could sell milk to the other mothers in the community, but she could never scrape up the $30 required to buy one. She considered borrowing the money, but the bank would not allow her to cross their threshold, even if she could afford their 100 percent annual interest. Alternatively, the local loan shark charged 40 percent per month.

In 2001, two years prior to my visit, she learned of a nongovernmental charitable organization named Zambuko Trust. Zambuko means *bridge*, signifying the bridge from poverty to hope. With affordable interest and no requirement for collateral, she borrowed $30 for six months to buy the cow that would give her life new hope. In gratitude, she named the cow Zambuko. Each day Zambuko produces the nutrients that help keep Esther, her sister, and their five children strong so they can maintain their grinding schedules. Enough milk was left over to sell to Esther's neighbors, which enabled her to make weekly loan payments.

When the loan for the cow was paid off, Esther borrowed another $75 to reestablish her vegetable farm. The money created work for the women she hired to prepare the soil and collect the brush that would serve as a hedge against animals and thieves. Finally, she planted covo seeds and began fertilizing the young plants that would soon sustain her family. Working alongside their mother (with their youngest sibling strapped to her back), the two older children quickly learned how to care for the cow and the garden. They are not yet aware how important this knowledge will be when Esther is gone, all too soon.

Communities like hers include virtually no men of working age, only boys and the elderly. Most of the few living young men have left the village for the cities in search of work. Widows and orphans learn to work together in pursuit of a common goal; they support each other like geese flying in formation.

We accompany Esther to the weekly meeting that she committed to attend as part of her loan agreement. Though almost all the women in the group are HIV-positive, it is not evident from their joyful exuberance and determination to succeed in their businesses. As at many traditional African gatherings, the women allot time for singing and dancing. Setting aside the multiple trials that burden them, they face this final unfair scourge with courage and resolve. I am as moved by the beauty of their open-air music, with its rich a cappella harmonies, as by any symphony in Chicago's Orchestra Hall.

When the women in loan groups meet each week and share experiences, they gain support and confidence in running their various enterprises. They know each other intimately. Each member of the group guarantees the other members' loans, giving them assurance that should one become incapacitated, the other women will cover her weekly payments and not burden her children with debt.

Every four or five months, after their loans are repaid, the women have the option of getting a larger loan to expand or diversify their businesses. These subsequent loans will not be granted until every member of the group completes her payments. Thus, if one of them is not able to make the weekly payment because of illness or some other legitimate crisis, the others chip in and make good on the loan. But if one member stops coming to the weekly meetings or tries to cheat the system, the other members visit her and pressure her to pay. With this level of peer support and accountability, repayment rates in these groups approach 100 percent.

Together Esther and her neighbors named their co-op the "Enjoyment Group." A few weeks prior to our visit, Esther's cow added to her enjoyment by giving birth to a calf. Her farm expanded, as did her hope. With her first two loans paid in full, Esther borrowed $250 to enlarge her garden as well as to purchase a brood of baby chicks. Every week Esther proudly reports her progress to the rest of the members.

The group leader continues to train them on how to improve their businesses. Members receive guidance in pricing and marketing, inventory control, and how to keep accurate records. By belonging to a co-op, the members are able to buy materials and supplies in bulk and to negotiate favorable prices.

From the co-op, Esther also learns much about her illness and how to care for herself. A health worker often attends the meeting, bringing additional information about how AIDS spreads, how to prevent it, and how to live a productive life once infected. With no access to medicine, let alone a cure, Esther eagerly absorbs all the techniques that may extend her life. Her dream is to establish her farm, nurture her children, and maintain her strength long enough for her oldest to carry on the business and care for the younger siblings after she is gone.

I listen as a health worker addresses Esther and the forty other women who have gathered for their weekly meeting. Peppered throughout her machine-gun presentation is the recurring theme that everyone should be tested for AIDS.

"Knowledge is power," she says. "As I stand here before you, I am HIV-positive. My husband was a soldier and he brought this to me. But as you can see, I am strong. Once I discovered my status, I improved my diet. Unfortunately, my child was born before I knew I was HIV-positive. Now the baby is also crippled by the disease."

She continues, "When you feel loved, you live longer, so don't reject those who are infected. It's not always wise to tell others if you're positive. Conserve your energy. Refrain from hard physical labor that will fatigue you. Avoid stress, since that will also sap your physical strength."

As I listen, I watch the women's faces in humble amazement. "How can they be so strong and joyful?" These women are impoverished and in want of medicine, but still they choose to experience the fullness of life. Is this another lesson that the working poor are teaching me? Their joy does not come from material wealth but from relationships and shared experiences, regardless of how bleak their lives might seem.

Esther's weekly loan-group meetings provide camaraderie. Gradually she discovers the hope that many with AIDS lack. Several times during our brief visit, Esther expresses her appreciation for the weekly meetings, where she receives not only financial assistance and business training, but also health training and invaluable support from other HIV-positive members.

With guidance from the health worker, support from her group, milk from her cow, eggs from her chickens, and fresh vegetables from her garden, Esther eats better and feels stronger. But she has also learned that to prolong her life she must minimize physical work and conserve her energy. How can she possibly follow that counsel when every day begins with three to four punishing hours of hauling water up a rugged hill?

I can sense her deep angst as she outlines her vision. "I have to carry so many buckets. If only I could buy a pump and some hoses, then I could stop making these many trips every morning." Esther elaborates on her dream, "I could expand the garden and grow more covo. And I'd gain several hours each day to sell my vegetables."

I did not want to squelch her enthusiasm but needed to ask the obvious question: "What makes you think there is water here?"

Esther had obviously been thinking about this and was ready with a response. "I know there is water near the ground. Others here in the valley, no closer than I am to the stream, have wells."

"And do you know how deep they had to drill in order to access the water?"

"They only dig some few meters. I've tested and it's here, too."

"And how do you operate this pump without any electricity in this valley?"

"We don't need electricity. The pump has two pedals that you push with your feet. It's not so difficult."

"What does a manual pump like the one you're describing cost?"

"Well, that's the problem. It's very expensive."

"What does that mean? How expensive?"

"Today, in U.S. dollars, the pump will cost about $350. But I also need to buy some short hoses, so I can get the water to my entire garden. And it would be good if I could have a little extra money to buy some fertilizer."

Consider the implication of what she just said. A small $400 loan could purchase and install a manual pump and fully equip this determined farmer. That small investment could mean the difference between life and death for Esther and her three children.

Her entrepreneur dreams do not end with a water pump or a farm. If she can live another six months and pay off the loan for a pump, she would borrow a couple hundred dollars to buy a sewing machine. "When I was a little girl my mother taught me to sew. I see other women in the co-op who make a good business with this."

Esther feels confident she could convert the skill into a lucrative enterprise. A simple pedal-operated machine and a few bolts of cloth are all it would take. "The children here must all wear uniforms to classes," she reminds me. "I've seen them, and I recognize that the demand for uniforms will remain as long as there are children. What's best is that I can teach this skill to my girls." In five years the oldest child will be thirteen and able to raise the others—if only Esther can prolong the inevitable and equip them to survive on their own. Noticing me mulling matters over in my mind, Esther chimes in with the same confident assessment she attributed to operating the pump, "It's not so difficult."

EVERYONE CAN DO SOMETHING

It's easy to look at countries like Zimbabwe, with their poverty and corrupt governments, and think there's no hope for people like Esther. But we can't let our frustration and despair immobilize us into inaction. What can individuals like you and me do to help bring justice to people like Esther? We can speak out against systems that perpetuate their poverty. We can tell their stories and make others aware of the day-to-day challenges they face. We can put pressure on our government to confront their country's leaders. We can live more simply to make more self-sustaining resources available. We can show the poor respect by thinking of them with admiration and anticipation instead of disdain or pity. We can wisely support the most effective and lasting solutions. We can avoid adding salt to their wounds by suggesting that they are poor as a result of their own doing. We can acknowledge that we are wealthy and that part of the reason is because we live where we do. That's a blessing over which we had no control. Surely doing justice includes leveling the playing field at least this much.

Esther did not want charity—just a fair chance to better her life and that of her family. From a poor working woman like Esther, I am learning that justice is not a handout, but a hand up—an act by someone with power or privilege to give those without power or privilege a chance. An opportunity. To do justice, then, is to do *something*. We cannot sit idly by when we see injustice. We can use whatever resources we have, including our spheres of influence, to provide others with a way out of their poverty. What we actually do will be different for each of us. But doing nothing will only allow injustice to flourish.

FAREWELL TO ESTHER

Before leaving Zimbabwe we visited the majestic Victoria Falls. Whenever I replay that scene I remember Esther. In my mind I've created a picture that symbolizes her life, one in which Esther is submerged in the water as it rushes ever faster toward the Falls. Powerfully and irrevocably, the water crashes over the immense cliff into a blinding mist. There is nothing I can do from the bank to rescue Esther from being carried over the edge. I imagine her calling out to me to protect her children and keep them from being swept into the deadly current like she was. Yearning for a brighter future for her family and others, I commit to do all I can to transform her hope into reality for mothers and children who face the devastation of AIDS.

In my imagination I speak to her: "Esther, born in Zimbabwe, you innocently entered the water when it was a gentle tributary. Streams quickly converged, rains fell, waters mounted, and you passed through many of life's rapids. Your place in the turbulent river is no more your doing than my place here on the secure bank is mine.

"We are sister and brother, created in the image of our loving Father. But I stand on the precipice admiring the beauty of the Falls, feeling the spray, while you are being swept away by the same waters that cool and refresh me. I cannot fully enter your world any more than I can invite you into mine.

"With no hint of self-pity, you have taught me much. Because of these fleeting moments when our paths crossed, I will never be the same. I marvel at the way you have prepared your children for the future. Now I promise to try and prevent children like them from falling into the river.

"I am honored to have been a part of your journey and to have played a small role in helping you endure. Someday we will gather our families together and dance to the song your group first sang to me near your home, near the narrow stream bridged with strategically placed stepping stones.

"Go in peace, Esther. Go knowing that with God's help you equipped your family well."

2

FAMILY

Healthy families, regardless of poverty, cultivate

dignity and become the foundation of society.

Thousands of families in poor countries live on garbage dumps. Garbage is to them what fertile soil is to farmers in Iowa—it is their scenery, their landscape. They were born on it, create their homes out of it, and will be buried under it. Families walk through it, play in it, and make a living from it. Garbage is their livelihood. Without garbage they have neither security nor identity.

Why would anyone live on a garbage dump? It's all part of the migration of rural poor to large cities, where they believe they will find work. Those cities with already inadequate infrastructures quickly become congested and overburdened. Like a fully saturated sponge, they cannot absorb the thousands of families eager to migrate to the bright lights, chasing promising tales with happy urban endings. Illiterate peasants full of dreams move with their families, only to find no jobs, no welcoming places to live. Soon they become part of the population living in squatter colonies, unable to afford land or negotiate a legitimate and secure lease. Every day they live in fear that their homes will be confiscated or demolished. Many are.

Every habitable inch becomes some family's dwelling place. With nowhere else to live, families set up housekeeping on the garbage dump. The camp begins at the base, where the garbage is aged and compacted.

As more settlers arrive, they spill up the sides of the heap where the refuse is fresher and the ground more spongy. After a while, little shacks cover the entire mountain of trash. Squatters create their one-room lean-tos from cardboard, plastic, or anything else they can recover from the debris. As they prosper, they use rusty sheets of corrugated iron to replace their plastic roofs, many of which are less than five feet above the ground. Then they replace cardboard floors with old wooden doors.

Eventually, entire villages of semi-permanent dwellings cling precariously to all sides of the dump. Only the summit of the dump is uninhabited, as that remains the fresh land awaiting tomorrow's refuse.

A DIFFERENT SMOKEY MOUNTAIN

By the early 1990s, Smokey Mountain had become the biggest active garbage "city" in the world. This infamous site, once on the outskirts of metro Manila, eventually consumed many city blocks and was surrounded for miles by tens of thousands of tiny shacks and enterprises. At that time almost half of metro Manila's population was living in squatter colonies; twenty-five thousand of the poorest of the poor ended up living in shanties on Smokey Mountain. These huts were so small that family members had to take turns sleeping.

I spent an afternoon several years ago walking the "streets" of Smokey Mountain. As I trudged through the narrow alleys, I noticed something that amazed me—something I wasn't really prepared for: these people were not living alone or isolated, but as families. Regardless of the size and condition of their makeshift hovels, inside were husband, wife, children, and sometimes elderly parents. These family members support each other, surviving on whatever they can salvage and resell.

Although I found the pervasive odor unbearable, for these families it was the scent of home. Perhaps the stench had escalated on the day of my visit from the hundred-degree temperatures and heavy rainfall of the night before. The smells of urine and decomposing waste began to burn my eyes as I walked through what felt like an eternal grove of Porta Potties on a muggy summer afternoon. In places, narrow planks and other micro-bridges enhanced the pathways, but for much of the time, I plodded through slushy debris, rotting food, and human feces. Here even the simple need to retie my shoelace became a loathsome burden.

With not a single shrub or tree growing, the only points of beauty in this drab garbage city were the sparkling eyes of the children. In several of the shelters, amid pervasive filth, mothers lovingly bathed their children in basins of water. In other shacks, freshly laundered clothes hung in the putrid air to dry. Even in this degrading neighborhood, people lived with dignity and attempted cleanliness, although the washing was only relatively effective. For some it consisted of bathing in the stagnant pond at the base of this mountain of rotting garbage. The oily liquid filtered through the waste, and in no time the hot sun left the clothes dry and at least somewhat cleaner than everything else around them.

What causes a man and a woman to leave their father and mother and cling to one another? To make love on the floor of a hovel only a couple yards away from another couple fighting in the middle of the night, with only two sheets of cardboard or cloth hanging between them? Why do they give birth on a garbage dump, and there love and protect their offspring? Why form a family and create a home in spite of so much hardship?

When you and I think of family, we probably think of Sunday dinners, kids playing in the backyard, Mom and Dad tucking a child into a warm, comfortable bed. But family isn't something Westerners dreamed up. Somewhere deep within each of us is a God-given impulse that yearns for love, desires independence, and craves family. These hardworking poor people were showing me that. In fact, they were teaching me lessons about my own family that I wish I had learned a lot earlier.

THE DILEMMA OF PLENTY

When our three children were in preschool I took on a second part-time job so I could provide better for our family, which basically meant more toys for the kids and new furniture for their parents. Up until then, our entire house had been furnished from garage sales we frequented during and right after college. Like most American men and women, I gave my family more stuff, but I robbed them of time together as a family.

In addition to the second job, I immersed myself in renovating our older home. I love remodeling and find it gratifying and energizing to convert dead space into something functional while also adding equity to the house. Every Saturday for many years, I would get up with the sun and work on house projects till midnight, pausing only long enough for a quick meal. Over the past twenty-five years, I have converted attics into bedrooms and playrooms, added decks and screened-in porches, built a family room addition, and created a rental unit in our basement, complete with bathroom.

I'm both proud and ashamed of these accomplishments, because I almost never involved our family in any of this creativity. I was so bent on making progress and concluding a venture that I failed to slow down and include those who would supposedly benefit from my diligence. As a result, our *house* was bigger and better, but our *home* was weaker and poorer.

The house we moved to when our son was a one-year-old and where we lived when his two younger sisters were born is a regrettable black hole that consumed me for six years. That house was an enjoyable forty-five minute train ride away from Chicago, a city with marvelous museums, exhibits, parks, beaches, concerts, and shows of all kinds. Yet I can count on my fingers and toes the number of excursions we took during those years to avail ourselves of the opportunities to build memories and add equity to our family.

One day we sold that house. While Lise and the children were outside preparing the car for our long drive to Georgia, I went back into the empty shell one last time to make sure we hadn't left anything behind and to turn off lights. On my way out, I paused in the living room to admire what we had created. The high ceilings that had once sagged were now flat and smooth. The old windows on either side of the fireplace that for years had been buried under aluminum siding on the outside and bookcases on the inside were now restored and invited the western sun into the room, bringing life to the oak floors that once had been covered by mustard-colored wall-to-wall carpeting. I admired again the mantel and trim I had spent months designing and building from scratch.

I leaned up against the ten-paned French doors I had discovered in the attic. I had spent weeks stripping, varnishing, and re-installing them between the living room and dining room. But instead of leaving with a sense of pride and accomplishment, as I rested my head against the mauve-painted door jamb, I could no longer see my handiwork through my tears. Waves of sorrow and regret washed over me as I looked at the fleeting achievements for which I had exchanged six years of my life. All those weekends and evenings I could have played Candy Land or gone to swing in the park, I had bartered for something temporal. Now the inevitable had come and I was bidding it all farewell. In that moment I realized that family is what I valued most, yet family is what I had blindly forfeited.

This was the '80s, about the time when young urban professionals began to be called "yuppies." Materialism was everywhere. Owning the right brand was everything. We all caught the virus. While we missed richness of spirit and value of family, we proved we cared about our babies by the brand of the strollers we pushed through the neighborhood. If anything, that virus is even more widespread today. Thankfully, life is about growth, and we can change. Visiting places like Smokey Mountain has taught me much about family.

Well-functioning families, regardless of poverty, cultivate dignity and become the foundation of nurturing societies. Irrespective of nationality or culture, the family structure offers protection and security. In family, people of all ages find emotional support and value. What astounds me is that wherever in the world I go, in whatever cultural or economic stratum I find myself, a high value is placed on the family unit. And while it would be grossly inaccurate to imply that poorer families are always harmonious and loving, when all you have is each other, you learn to value each other above all else.

A METROPOLIS BUILT ON GARBAGE

Thankfully, no one lives on the dumps near Manila anymore. The Philippine government tries to better manage both its garbage and the needs of those who used to live on top of it. Payatas is a controlled disposal facility owned and operated by the Philippine government. Covering more than twenty acres, the garbage reaches as high as a ten-story building. This colossal facility receives some five hundred dump trucks each day. Before being escorted out to the dump to view the process firsthand and to meet the people working there, our group heard an informative presentation from the former military colonel who runs the operation.

"We have a power plant here at Payatas that is fueled by methane," the colonel began. "As the garbage decomposes, it releases this highly flammable gas. The methane channels through plastic pipes to a generator, where it converts into electricity that provides light to most of the 2.3 million residents of Castle City—a bedroom community on the foothills of the dump that provides housing for those who either work on it or in one of the thousands of enterprises surrounding it." He explained the health and safety hazards. "No one lives here, and we strictly enforce a nine o'clock curfew."

Instead, young men from the surrounding communities show up when the gates open every morning at four o'clock and the first of five hundred trucks begin to file in. Waiting at the gate, they scramble onto the moving vehicles and sort through the trash. They have only fifteen minutes while the driver passes inspection, completes paperwork, and heads toward the dump. Once they reach the end of the road, they jump down and run back to the gate where they wait for the next truck.

During this first step of the recycling process, approximately half of each truck's contents gets thrown over the side and is gathered up by fellow scavengers who quickly separate it for recycling. Metal, plastic, glass, cardboard, and rubber are sorted during this initial phase.

The trucks then rumble down the long dirt roadway before heading up to the designated location for this particular day's delivery. Hundreds of scavengers will be waiting when the trucks arrive on top of the dump where the garbage is delivered and somewhat spread out by the trucks. The debris is available to this second set of scavengers for only twenty minutes, after which it is bulldozed into the towering mound and becomes inaccessible.

On one occasion I noticed an exchange erupting between one of the scavengers and the driver of an enormous yellow bulldozer. The machine approached the most recent shipment of raw material and those still sifting through it. Like David confronting Goliath, one scavenger stood his ground, made eye contact with the driver, pointed to his wrist and communicated clearly that the twenty minutes were not up yet. The driver then turned off the engine, propped his feet on the dash, and lit a cigarette. The scavenger went right back to work, separating out the plastic milk cartons, tin cans, yesterday's newspapers, and glass bottles. Placing each item in one of several large nylon bags, he organized the trash for resale and recycling.

Here, entire families—men and women, the elderly, and children of all ages—poke through the trash looking for anything of value. With no shelter from the sun or rain, they squat, many of them with nothing protecting their feet other than perhaps the most primitive sandals. A few wear gloves, but most dig barehanded through the rusty metal and broken glass.

Castle City evolved from the Payatas facility along with microenterprises of all kinds available to support the families who live and work there. Houses double as storefronts for every conceivable product or service. Children at both primary and secondary levels attend the Castle City public schools. Roaming dogs are plentiful and mangy. Churches serve the faithful of a variety of traditions, the most common being Roman Catholic. Homes consist of no more than one- or two-room shacks made from concrete blocks and covered by corrugated iron sheets. Separated from neighbors by only a few feet, these dwellings are only a minor improvement over the squatters' former hovels on the dump.

We passed a health clinic as a young couple approached, walking down the dusty street. They carried an infant wrapped in the blanket presented at birth, presumably only days previously. Noting the simple facility and impoverished surroundings, I was reminded of the holy family in Bethlehem; born in a stable and raised in the family of a poor Jewish carpenter under Roman rule, Jesus too knew racism, injustice, and want.

As I walked past the young couple, we exchanged smiles—theirs, happy to see the rare foreigner in their neighborhood; mine, to camouflage my grief. Dozens of naked children frolicked in one of the wider main streets that looked more like a murky river than a road. I watched as they jumped and splashed in a six-inch–deep puddle, about ten feet by twenty feet. The stagnant cesspool had obviously been there for days, the lowest spot on the road, collecting everything from runoff to dishwater to sewage, and anything in between.

Emotionally distraught by the congestion and living conditions in Castle City, I also was encouraged, in the midst of the squalor, by the strong and loving families I met. To be sure, not every resident is part of a happy marriage or a functional family. But each of the four families I spent time with that day added their own expression of dedication, creating a beautiful patchwork of supportive and secure relationships.

FAMILIES THAT WORK TOGETHER

As I describe my visits to the dumps of Manila, where so many families work together on the garbage mountains or in homegrown factories in Castle City, you might think I'm advocating a return to child labor. I'm not. But one lesson I learned from the poor about family is the value of working together toward a common goal. Sadly, the goal of most of these families was survival. I could not help but think how we in the West try to shelter our kids from whatever challenges we face, while these parents do just the opposite. Here in Castle City, it's as if the mom or dad says to the kids, "We're poor, but there's nothing wrong with that. We'll all work together and things will get better." In many cases, things *do* get better and the entire family benefits.

Consider the Davao family, whose home also functions as their little family factory. Mom, dad, and five children—ranging in age from seven to fourteen—all work together. For the past ten years the family has woven plastic baskets that they sell to stores nearby or directly to individuals in the outdoor market. They buy used nylon bands from the recycling plant near the dump. The three-quarter-inch–wide strapping costs them thirty cents per pound, and comes in red, orange, yellow, blue, and white. Whenever there's a shortage of these used strips, they supplement them with new material they buy for $3 a roll, enough for ten baskets. The new flexible plastic is easier to work with and faster to weave, but it is also more expensive and erodes what little profit the baskets yield.

When we arrived at the Davao home one afternoon, the five children and both parents were working side-by-side, weaving baskets of different sizes. At first, I was concerned about seeing the children at work, not at school. Then our host explained to me that the schools around the dump run in two shifts, from six a.m. to noon, and then from noon until six p.m.

"The Davao children are enrolled for the school's morning session," our host explained. "Each afternoon they spend three or four hours weaving. By working together, the seven family members produce more than twenty of these brightly colored baskets each day."

On the one hand, I recognized that these children's lives were far from ideal. They live in a very difficult environment. I don't know how much time they have to play and just be kids, or whether working long days has affected their ability to pay attention in school. Our translator also explained that there are some days when the children are needed to work longer hours and miss classes. But on the other hand, I couldn't help but think that in addition to adding to their family's income, each child is also gaining the self-esteem that comes from honest work. In previous generations, American teens frequently helped out on the family farm or were gainfully employed elsewhere to supplement the family income. That helped bond the family together. In today's culture, with most teens doing neither, we have to work harder to keep our teenagers engaged with the family and to help them feel valued, needed, and loved.

"Who really is richer?" I wondered. "The young people who work and contribute to the family or those who never have?"

Those options are not debated among the families I encountered in and around the garbage dumps of Manila. With a series of microloans, the Davaos expanded their family business and increased their profits. Starting out with a $70 loan two years ago, they are now paying back their fourth loan of $200. The influx of working capital allowed them to buy more recycled material in bulk. They have since hired five other women in the community who are paid by the piece to make baskets at their homes. In addition to increasing income for the Davao family, this expansion created employment for other mothers who were unable to work outside their homes.

"The Davaos have recently started exporting their baskets," our host boasts. "One of their relatives married a Kuwaiti who opened a channel, and they now sell more than one hundred baskets per month in Kuwait."

As I watched them weave I kept thinking, "What a resourceful and close-knit family. These young children may lack the security of possessions, but they have no shortage of security within their family."

Though I was well aware of the serious disadvantages of raising a family in Castle City, I left the Davaos' home pondering some of the advantages. How many parents have daily blocks of uninterrupted time to instill in their children their values, work ethic, and view of God and the world? We work hard at raising our children to be independent and self-reliant. We, too, could benefit by finding productive ways to spend concentrated time together creating deep bonds and sharing values.

ENTERPRISE IN PAYATAS DUMP AND CASTLE CITY

Back to the dump and more lessons on family. Deborah Talong grew up and had initially been rearing her three children on a dump that collapsed. That horrific tragedy, in which hundreds of people were buried alive, led to improvements like the establishment of Castle City, where this family now resides. Several years ago, Deborah received a loan to start a business. With her first loan of about $50 she purchased recycled material that she and her children used to make doormats and seat pads. Rolling the material into cylinders about the thickness of a hot dog, they would then coil the cloth tubes round and round like a cinnamon bun and stitch them tightly together. She sold the round pads, about eighteen inches in diameter, as chair cushions for a couple of dollars apiece. Using the same method and recycled materials, the family also produced oval doormats that varied in price depending on the size.

Every week Deborah dutifully attended the credit center meeting, making her payment on principal, interest, and savings. There she also received business training and support from the other female loan clients. Every four to six months, when she paid off her loan, she'd take out a slightly larger one and expand her business by purchasing more material and hiring others to help produce the rugs. After a few loan cycles the members of her center elected her as one of their officers.

Along with several other advanced entrepreneurs, she was offered an upgraded loan product and was able to access larger loans with no requirement to attend the weekly meetings. With her new flexibility, more favorable loan requirements, and her recent loan of $2,000, Deborah's business continued to grow. She now involves ten families in her sewing business, and each day produces three hundred little rugs. Advertising is limited to word of mouth, and her distribution channels consist of department stores, the shoe market, and other middlemen. She gets her goods to market with a small motorcycle and two vans that she bought from the profits of the business. In total, Deborah employs about one hundred people, some in sales and others in shipping and delivery. After paying them, buying her material, and covering her operating costs, she earns a net profit between $600 and $1,000 per month.

As volume grew, Deborah graduated from purchasing recycled cloth at the dump to buying scraps and remnant material from factories, where she also gathered rejected sewing thread. As she told me of the developments in her business, I was surprised to learn how world economics and politics affect even fledgling enterprises in remote communities. With the events of 9/11 and the downturn in the U.S. economy, the factories where Deborah bought her scrap materials came to a near standstill. The remnants she depended on were no longer available, forcing her to cut back production to weather that temporary storm.

This intimidating side effect of globalization could have put Deborah under, but instead it fueled this tenacious entrepreneur's prosperity. It is clear that one of the keys to her achievement is her commitment to the high quality of her products. "Now I export rugs to China and Korea," she proudly told me. "But I don't see myself as successful yet. I dare not rest on the accomplishments of the past." In addition to excellence, Deborah is also committed to her employees; here, the term *family* takes on new meaning. At her home, where most of the products are made, her workers are not only free to use her flushing toilet, but also allowed to take showers, two luxuries available to only a few at this level of society. I sensed her delight in the arrangement when she exclaimed, "We all eat together like one big family!"

In my mind, however, Deborah's crowning achievement was not the success of her business in the face of international impediments. Nor was it the jobs she had created for one hundred members of her community. Rather, it was how this woman, who grew up as a squatter on a garbage dump, had miraculously broken the cycle of poverty in just one generation.

And those children who worked alongside their mom making mats from recycled refuse? "My oldest child received a scholarship from the Department of Science and Technology," she boasted. "He will soon graduate from college." Because he learned the value of hard work from his mother, he and his own future family will have a better life. Isn't that the best gift any parent can give a child?

DAILY FAMILY REUNIONS

Over and over again during my visit to Castle City, I saw the kind of family ties that many of us in the West covet. For example, I met one family where three generations lived together in three tiny adjacent houses, each smaller than my garage. That living arrangement was not unusual. The oldest generation, a couple about fifty years old, lived in the middle house with their unmarried daughter. They took us around back and showed us the pens where they had once raised about thirty pigs. "For many years this piggery supported our entire family," the mother told us. "But several years ago my husband was seriously injured in an automobile accident. We had to sell all the pigs to pay for his hospitalization."

Although the pens are empty, the family hopes someday to save enough capital to buy more pigs. In the meantime, while the father is healing, his wife supports them through a carry-out food business. "I prepare the food here in our kitchen," she said, pointing to a corner of the one-room house, "and my daughter helps sell the hot meals to our neighbors." In addition, she assists her other two adult daughters, who live with their respective families on either side of the parents, to make and sell baskets from recycled plastic straps (as do the Davaos).

In Castle City I was heartened by the practical love this extended family showed each other. When tragedy struck, the family came together because they had no other safety net. They supported and defended each other and demonstrated an enviable closeness. Now they pool their resources with the dream of restoring the family business.

All the while they live and grow together, building lasting bonds that will carry them through unexpected sorrows and joys.

By contrast, despite my relative wealth and mobility, I have little contact with my brothers and sister, and my children are even less connected with their twenty-some cousins or any of their grandparents. For most of their lives, we have lived more than a thousand miles from our nearest relative. I left home at eighteen, traveled ten thousand miles away to attend college, and quickly learned to manage without siblings or parents.

In our affluent and mobile society we have to be intentional about relationships lest we lose the value of extended family. Thankfully, my two daughters have settled near us. I am grateful for cell phones, email, webcams, and relatively inexpensive air travel that enable Lise and me to stay close to our son who lives in New York. He, too, continues to work at maintaining intimacy despite the miles. Underneath I think we all yearn for family ties that are "up close and personal." Physical connectedness, security, and shared values are easier to maintain in the developing world, and therefore seem far more prevalent.

SACRIFICING FOR FAMILIES

I learned another lesson about families in Castle City, one that I'm still trying to assimilate. It came from another unforgettable woman, Jody Caceres, whose story is similar to the others but with an almost shocking twist. A physically small woman at only four and a half feet, her spirit looms large, so much so that the twenty other women in her business cooperative elected her as their president.

"All four of my children are in school," Jody said with pride. Her three daughters—ages fourteen, ten, and eight—attended one of the public schools in Castle City, and she had recently enrolled her six-year-old son in preschool. Like several other women I met in her credit center, Jody used her loan to purchase plastic strips that she wove into baskets.

"My husband is a family driver and security guard," she told me. I think she meant that he was a chauffeur for a wealthy family, but the way she rolled her eyes when referring to him implied there was much more to the story. Based on what little she did say, I could only guess he was not much help in providing for the children.

If the family unit is a near-universal phenomenon, it is equally undeniable that in developing countries the woman still does the heavy lifting in nurturing the family. Typically, she is responsible to feed, clothe, educate, discipline, and maintain the physical and emotional health of the children. In many agrarian cultures, she has the additional burden of tilling the land and harvesting the crops.

Forty years ago, when microenterprise development was first introduced in the developing world, almost all the loans were made to men. Over time this trend has reversed, as women have not only proven to be better credit risks but have routinely demonstrated they are better equipped and motivated to use the profits of the business to care for the family.

I am grateful that Jody is one of them, because I enjoyed her company and her enriching insights. Jody helped me understand the economics of the basket business in which these women are engaged. "A roll of plastic straps costs three dollars," she told me. "I make ten baskets with it. Some big and some little."

This means, on average, she invests thirty cents in raw material in each basket. "How long do you work on one basket?" I asked her.

"About one hour, sometimes two. It depends on size and design," she replied with a proud grin, similar to the one that came across her face when she reported that all her children attend school.

I calculated that in a good long day she can make ten baskets. "Where do you sell them?" I asked.

"Mostly I sell to the grocery stores and supermarkets for about sixty-five cents each," Jody explained. "I also sell some from my house for ninety cents."

I did the mental arithmetic. Subtracting the cost of her raw material, at best she makes thirty-five to sixty cents per hour—three to six dollars for a long day. That assumes she sells everything she makes, and doesn't include anything for marketing and selling. Jody also employs several others.

"I have seven mothers who live near me. They work at their houses. I pay them ten cents for a small basket and up to twelve or thirteen for a big one."

"Okay," I thought. "She reduces her profit by an average of eleven cents, but she makes up for it in volume. The women's labor gives them some income while they are at home raising their children. But their earnings from one basket still can't buy a daily allotment of rice for one child, or pay the round-trip bus fare to school for that single child."

After mentally doing the numbers and confirming that I understood them correctly, I probed at a deeper level. I wanted this bright woman's thoughts. "Jody, what value do these women place on their children's lives that make them so desperate they will work for eleven cents an hour?"

Jody may have been self-conscious in earlier conversations, covering her teeth as she giggled, but this time she was not the least bit uncomfortable with my question. Even though it was clear she understood, she didn't answer. She didn't have to. Instead, looking deep into my eyes, she simply nodded as if to say, "You get the picture. I am glad that someone from the outside understands our situation. Now, go speak for us."

During our conversation, Jody casually mentioned that she had graduated from college. Wondering if I understood that part of our conversation correctly, I later asked her loan officer if she did in fact earn a college degree.

"Yes," she assured me, "and she used to have a coveted office job. She even had air conditioning!"

I was stunned. Later, when I asked Jody why she was now staying at home making baskets, her reply was matter-of-fact: "For my kids." This enterprising woman, raised in poverty, educated and equipped to enjoy a better life for herself, chooses to live in relative poverty to be at home with her children during their formative years.

What lesson do I take from Jody's decision not to work outside her home? Perhaps instead of falling into traps of dogmatic philosophy, we should view such choices through a pragmatic lens focused on family needs. Jody taught me that family comes first—even ahead of her own personal comfort, even ahead of a better living environment for her children. If giving them a nicer home meant leaving them all day, it wasn't an option for her. Sometimes we justify our absence from our families because we think we are providing them with a better, more comfortable life.

Certainly that was the case when I took a second job and spent the rest of my time remodeling our home. I regret I did not follow Jody's model, remembering that there are seasons when our children's need for support and nurture trumps everything else.

WE ALL HAVE OUR GARBAGE

As much as I value the lessons I learned about family from these hospitable people in Manila, I can't say I enjoyed my time there—at least not on the dumps. Even on a good day, dumps are smelly, depressing places, but the people I met were anything but depressed. That's the paradox. Those who have improved their lives, by their entrepreneurial skills and a few small loans, still must make their homes in the midst of their fellow citizens' garbage.

By contrast, families in the West—rich in material possessions— often live on a different kind of dump, one surrounded by impoverished relationships, fractured families, and the heartbreak that goes with both. Though poor families are not immune to these disappointments, the courageous families I met in the slums of Manila highlight the risks bred by wealth when we overemphasize values like independence and materialism. While Western wealth can purchase substitutes and distractions, it cannot buy more time with family, more love and respect for parents, more self-confidence for teenagers, or more dignity for the elderly. While poor families aren't inherently more loving or without struggles, I am a far richer man for witnessing the importance that the poorest of the poor place on family.

As I write this chapter, I am once again embarking on a major house renovation. This time, however, I have chosen not to become so absorbed in the project that I let it take me away from my family. Left to my own stubborn devices, I would climb up a ladder and put even more distance between myself and the people I love. In the past I justified my actions by saying I was doing it for them. That is how many of us rationalize our disconnectedness. Families don't need more stuff to function properly. They need each other.

My situation is not the same as the working poor. My family is not in a position to have to work for our very survival. For this, I am grateful. I am blessed to have the means to hire someone to work on our house.

But I am finally learning how to apply one rich lesson from the families I have met and admired in the developing world. Instead of getting caught up in activities and material things that don't last, I will spend time with my family today, sharing a picnic together. We'll tell our stories, laugh, and simply enjoy each other's presence.

3

COMMUNITY

People in the developing world wholly embrace,

participate in, and are enriched by community.

If I described the contents of my garage, you might deduce that I live in the country, miles from my nearest neighbor. Or you might conclude that I just like to collect stuff. Why else would I have my own lawn mower, snow blower, hedge clipper, weed whacker, tree trimmer, leaf blower, and about every other tool and gadget to maintain my house and yard? I don't live in the country. I live in a somewhat densely populated suburb with neighbors on all sides of me. And guess what? Inside their garages are almost identical models of the same tools and machines I own.

Wouldn't it make sense to call an informal powwow with my neighbors and make a few executive decisions? "Jim, I'll buy a leaf blower, you buy a hedge trimmer, Mary can get a weed whacker, and Steve will provide the snow blower." Then when I need to trim the grass close to the fence, I can borrow from Mary who, in turn, can come get my leaf blower when she needs it.

It might make sense, but despite living in a charming neighborhood with kind neighbors, we haven't had that powwow yet. In fact, we purchase these duplicate tools so we *never* need to borrow from our neighbors. You know what I'm talking about. We feel lucky to talk to our neighbors, let alone borrow from them.

I recently attended the last few hours of a block party with other families on our street. The first thing I noticed was the incredible number of children at the party. When we moved into this house eleven years earlier, only two children other than ours lived on the block. Who were these kids, whom did they belong to, and when did they all arrive?

I met two couples that day for the first time, each with two or three kids. They live within a hundred yards of our front door. It might have been understandable that I didn't know their names if they had recently moved in, but both families had been living in the neighborhood almost as long as we had.

Compared to the desperately poor people I have met all over the developing world, we in the West are virtual hermits who might as well be living on isolated islands in the middle of the ocean. We live next to each other and we might wave as we get into our cars for the commute to work, but that's just about it when it comes to the practice of community. The working poor are teaching me a valuable lesson about community that is crystal clear: not only do you get more done when you work together, but you receive the added blessings of friendship and camaraderie.

PLAYING TOGETHER IN THE SANDBOX

Community is something we "unlearn." Just watch young kids at the playground. They scurry about in little groups, climbing on the equipment or playing in the sandbox. A new kid shows up and the group makes room for him or finds a spot on the team for her. As parents, we teach our youngsters to share. When they do, we think it's cute. Then when we become adults, we develop that rugged individualism that quickly leads us to erect barriers between ourselves and our neighbors. The poor cannot afford such self-sufficiency. To put it more positively, they have learned that community—working together, sharing their possessions as well as their friendship— enriches their lives.

The working poor do just about everything together. I recall going to a small village in India to visit a community center. I made my way through a maze of dirt paths, chaos, and debris until I came to a sewage-filled rut that led to the center, a small square building with no curtains, no ceiling, no carpet, and only the faded memory of paint.

Every week, two dozen women gather in the single-room building. They do not own property, pay taxes, carry a driver's license, or possess a birth certificate. These women are squatters living near the lowest rung of the economic ladder. The only ones lower are homeless street people. Officially, these women don't exist. Unofficially, they are business owners; they are the movers and shakers in their town of thousands of similar squatters.

Each woman is a source of bright color in this drab place, clothed in a uniquely striking sari: crimson with gilded flowers, silver with sapphire stripes, royal blue with a sheen that ripples with movement. Most of the women are younger than I might expect for a group formed only ten years ago. At the weekly meetings they recite their list of vows in unison: they will deal honestly in their businesses, keep their homes clean, send their children to school, support other members in their group, boil their water. They also pray together. Quite unfettered by the fact that some are Christians and most are Hindu, they ask God to bless their businesses and to show mercy to their families.

I suspect I am the first Westerner ever to enter this one-room building. The women's initial curiosity quickly evaporates as they continue updating each other on progress and problems in their varied home enterprises. I join them, sitting cross-legged on the concrete floor.

Through my interpreter, Said (who is also the executive director of the organization that provided their business loans), I am invited to interact with the members. I ask them questions about their group and what membership in the co-op means to them. Some talk about the businesses they have been able to start with their first $25 or $50 loans. Most of the conversation on this particular day, however, is focused not on the individuals but on the incredible results they have accomplished as a group.

The little room in which we sit is a good example, one of the women tells me. Until a few years ago, it was the location of the local garbage dump; not the official dump site, but simply the place where everyone agreed to toss garbage. Very little is discarded by the impoverished of the world, but over time, the mound began spilling into the walkways.

Meanwhile, weekly village meetings were held under a nearby tree since no home was large enough for all the participants.

When they learned of a new government program designed for subsidized housing, the women petitioned the local officials to clear the trash from the site and to provide materials for the building in exchange for some of the labor involved in its construction. It worked!

Other success stories follow. A smiling member boasts of how the group lobbied together to secure postal service to their neighborhood for the first time. (I don't know how anyone delivers mail to houses without numbers, on paths with no names, for residents with no legal identity.) Another tells how the group banded together and persuaded the city to build a block of communal toilets in an open field that had once been used for the same purpose, without facilities. But the proudest moment, they tell me, is when they brought electricity to their village. Their joy is infectious as they recount the process.

For years their village survived with no access to electric power. Out of desperation, many of the residents leeched off of the system by connecting wires from their homes to a lone utility pole, creating a dense tangle of strands weaving in every direction. Despite their pleas to village officials, their poverty afforded them no more political clout than a cell of convicted felons. Finally, the women signed a petition and shared their case with the local newspaper. Someone from the paper took a photograph of the utility pole and published an article describing the dangerous plight of these squatters. In short order, the city sent a crew, corrected the chaotic pole, and ran an electric current to every home in that squatter village. The women proudly unfold a yellowed newspaper clipping, complete with photo. The power *of* community brought power *to* their community.

After the members recount all they have achieved as a group, twenty-five-year-old Menika, vice president of the group, leads them to the next item on their agenda, the all-important moment they have been eagerly anticipating. They have agreed ahead of time that today they will request additional credit for their expanding enterprises. Menika is to be their voice. It is not often that the executive director of the main office comes to their weekly meeting, and never an outsider like me—someone who must be dripping with limitless wealth. After all, my brand-name gym shoes cost more than any of them earns in several months—not to mention my watch, my camera, or my leather shoulder bag.

In no time, Menika and Said are engaged in a heated discussion as the rest of the sorority spontaneously cheers her on. Occasionally, after a loud group eruption, Said interrupts their debate long enough to interpret what has just been said so I can follow the gist of the conversation.

"The group needs the next round of credit, and would like larger loans this time so we can expand our businesses," Menika says forcefully.

"I'm sorry," Said replies, "but as you know, the next disbursement cannot be made until all the previous loans have been paid back in full."

"Except for two of us, everyone has paid back all the money that we borrowed, plus the interest we owed."

"That's commendable, but not good enough. No one gets more credit until the entire group pays in full."

"We understand the requirements, but you know what happened. One of the members bought a milk cow with her loan and the cow died."

"That's most unfortunate, but we had strongly recommended she use part of her loan to take out insurance on the cow."

Menika thrusts both her arms in Said's direction. "Well, she didn't! And now without milk to sell, how can you possibly expect her to pay off her loan?"

After the meeting, Said tells me the significance of his heated exchange with Menika and how delighted he was with their dialogue. He explained that when this now-dynamic young woman first came into the office less than two years ago to apply for a loan, she could not look him in the eye. Her poor self-esteem was evident as she gazed at the ground. She was unable to stand erect or raise her head. Now, with the success of her business and the support of her group, she has risen to this position of leadership where she is boldly making demands on behalf of the others. (Typically when a default on one member's loan is not intentional fraud, all the members chip in from their savings, so that members are eligible for new and larger loans, including the person who defaulted. The delinquent member repays her neighbors.)

After the group adjourns, we go with this remarkable woman to see her business and meet her family. Menika lives in a tiny two-room house, approximately 120 square feet in total, no larger than one of the smaller bedrooms in my home in the United States. One of her rooms serves as her place of business and kitchen during the day, and the place where Menika and her elderly mother sleep at night. The other room is home to Menika's brother, his wife, and their four children. Menika is the only breadwinner for the entire household of eight.

She introduces me first to her mother. Chronic hunger and premature aging have left her with a frail, drooping seventy-pound frame. All that is left of the colorful dot between her clouded eyes is a faded gray tattoo. I listen through Said as Menika's mother recounts this family's plight. In the past, Menika's brother had supported the family by working in a factory. Although his wages were low, it was enough money to provide one meal each day for his mother, wife, children, and three sisters. In time, the inhumane conditions in the sweatshop eroded his health, finally leaving him so weak he could no longer work. He was laid off, and with no safety net, all three generations faced utter destitution.

Menika's two older sisters had also been living in the little house at that time, sharing the room with Menika and their mother. Incapable of coming up with a dowry, they were unwanted as wives and had been unable to find work themselves. The two girls took the only action they knew to help their impoverished family—they doused each other with kerosene and lit themselves on fire.

Yes, you read that correctly. It was from this dark backdrop that Menika had first approached Said two years earlier. At that time he was the group's loan officer. She had figured out how much she needed to borrow and how she would repay the debt. Though small to us, to her the loan was, and still is, an astronomical amount, a significant risk. Timidly, as Said recounted to me, with shoulders drooping and head downcast, she asked to borrow a little less than $100. Menika explained the equivalent of her business plan to Said. He asked many difficult questions, but helped her complete an application.

Within a couple of weeks an agreement was signed and she received the funds to buy a wet-grinder. Grinding rice by hand is a tedious and physically taxing chore that many families would gladly pay a few rupees to eliminate. Therein lies Menika's business. Each day her neighbors bring their rice for her to grind, some paying in rupees and others with rice. Content with either, her investment and business secures at least one daily meal for her entire family.

After six months, she had paid off the loan; now she uses the income to send her brother's four children to school. Someday, in her old age, with no husband or children of her own and no welfare program for the elderly, maybe one of them will take her in.

Today Menika supports her extended family. Later they will care for her. She leads her co-op now, but soon another leader will rise up and serve her. Prior to her involvement, the group brought electricity to her home, and perhaps under her watch they will all enjoy running water.

This is how the poor do things. Out of necessity, they learn the richness of community.

COWBOYS OR COMMUNITY MEMBERS?

Here in the West we don't have the same motivation to discover community. Perhaps unintentionally, at times we exchange community for independence, privacy, mobility, and opulence. With our wealth, we build fences around our homes to protect our possessions and privacy. What I have learned about community from the poor is that we are missing out on tremendous benefits.

During our thirty-five years together, my wife and I have never lived near family. When our first child was born, we joined a small group of five other couples from our church, each with young families. During our regular get-togethers we would make a point of sharing our personal struggles and joys. That camaraderie lasted less than two years before Lise and I relocated to the western suburbs of Chicago. Though fewer than fifty miles away from those friends, we might as well have moved to Africa. Within a year's time we had almost entirely stopped seeing them.

Soon, craving the intimacy of the earlier group, we formed another group of four couples, none of whom we had previously known. We met together faithfully every week, taking turns preparing dinner, hosting, and leading meaningful discussion. Then another move left us again feeling alone and adrift. Although I maintained a very deep friendship with one of those men for several more years, a tragic accident took his life.

My point is that in our culture we have to seek out community in a deliberate manner. Unlike the world's working poor, we do not depend on community for survival. Many of the poor live among the same people for an entire lifetime—often for generations. In our culture we can keep our secrets, controlling much of what our neighbors learn about us. To some extent we can choose what façade to present to the world, and with only superficial connections, it's not hard to keep it up. It's as if our culture, particularly the men of my generation, have watched too many cowboy movies and have believed the recurring theme: *Go West, young man.* Leave everyone behind. Real men don't need others. A couple six-shooters, tough leather chaps, and a good horse are all the friends you need. Most of us would say we've outgrown the romantic, John Wayne notion of individualism, but without knowing it, we cling to its false message of freedom.

MARGARITA AVILA'S BET ON COMMUNITY PAYS OFF

One thing I love about communities in the developing world is the way in which the poor reach out to others. As I discovered in South America, when you have benefited from community, you want to widen its influence.

Dug into small caverns along the hillside of Bogotá, Colombia, are hundreds of little shacks with tin front walls only. When the rains come, the water gushes down the slopes and floods these homes, bringing with it mud, sewage, and illness. For children growing up here, sickness is as much the norm as Beanie Babies and vitamin supplements were for my children.

Margarita Avila lives in one of these shacks carved into a recess of the cliff. She joined a trust group with other women in her village and borrowed about $100 to open a little beauty shop to serve other women living on the side of the mountain. As volunteer treasurer of their group, Margarita was aware of how much members had accumulated through their weekly savings program. She also became aware of a family of eight in their village, Juanita Tolosa's family, who were suffering from illness and hunger and surviving in a dirt-floored tin shack under a concrete bridge. Margarita used the weekly trust group meeting to collect food from the members for Juanita Tolosa and her children.

As necessary as the donated food was, Margarita knew from her own experience that what Juanita Tolosa needed most was an opportunity to earn money to add to her husband's meager income. The following week at the trust group meeting, Margarita reported on what she had learned, asking the others if they would allow Juanita Tolosa to become a member of their group. Several members initially resisted. They worried that Juanita Tolosa might be too much of a risk, and if she didn't pay back her loan, the group would be held responsible. What if Juanita Tolosa used the money for medicine or food rather than as capital for a business? What if she herself became ill and couldn't work?

Margarita reminded them that when several of them had been unable to make a weekly payment in the past, the others had chipped in to cover for them that week. After considerable debate, the group agreed to take $70 from their combined savings and extend it as a personal loan to Juanita Tolosa.

With the money, Juanita Tolosa purchased material to make popular plastic cabinets, a simple type of modular furniture. Soon she was earning $6 per day, enough to pay for her daughter's diabetes treatment. With this addition to her husband's income, the family was eating three meals a day. Juanita Tolosa did not miss a single loan payment, and when the debt was paid off a few months later, the group celebrated her triumph and invited her to join as an official member of their trust group.

GRIEVING TOGETHER

When I recall how this group of people reached out to a family struggling with an illness, I can't help but contrast this story with one of my own. Several years ago my younger brother, Randy, died of cancer. After attending his funeral in another city, I returned home to my community, a neighborhood oblivious to my sorrow. No one on our street felt my pain. I had been away, but nobody knew it or why. I grieved at the thought of not seeing Randy again, never to be challenged by his probing questions and well-informed opinions. No one even knew I'd had a brother, let alone that he had died. I can't blame them, because like most everyone in my neighborhood, I kept to myself. My brother died and no one in my community grieved with me. That would be inconceivable in the developing world.

When his adventurous and faith-filled life came to an abrupt halt, Randy left behind his wife, Bonnie, and three daughters who were living in a Muslim country. In the Middle East, where Randy and his family had lived for the past twenty years, a natural community had formed around them. They intentionally limited their contact with Westerners and chose to live in a lower-income neighborhood, sending their children to public schools.

In that environment the custom calls for a forty-day period of grieving, during which time friends and neighbors drop by unannounced, pay their respects, and express their love. During those six weeks, Bonnie rarely left their apartment. Friends from all over the country, and residents from their neighborhood, some of whom they had never met, came to show their concern and extend community. The majority of the guests were Muslims, undeterred by Bonnie's overt Christian faith. I admit to a fair amount of envy as I read her account of how her community responded:

> I am struck by the differences in how my two cultures handled death and mourning. I realized firsthand the principle in the Middle Eastern culture that it is very important not to leave someone alone when they are ill or suffering, but in the U.S. leaving people alone, letting them have privacy, is seen as more considerate.

> In my adopted culture, according to tradition, the family of the deceased stays at home for several weeks after a death. Within forty days close friends and family as well as neighbors, friends, people from our national church, etc., are expected to visit them many times. We kept track of all who came, and within three weeks we had more than four hundred visitors.

> Fortunately, a dear friend of mine moved in during those weeks and was on hand to make the countless cups of tea and coffee required, to serve sweetmeats, cookies, and fruit that had been brought. I laid out pictures of my husband's final days, his funeral, and burial, to help them process the stark fact that he would not be returning. It gave those who had especially loved him some closure of their own. Because he had left looking relatively healthy five months before, it was hard for them to realize his death.

> Neighbors came together in groups. There were often women I

barely knew, but who had watched us carefully from afar, and were impressed with what they saw. They came and sat in the living room, gently asking me all about the illness and death. I found that even though it was sometimes wearying to repeat the story again and again, there was nothing I wanted to talk about more. It was healing to share, to explain, to have people want to hear, to remember good days and fond memories. Sometimes we wept silently together, sometimes we chuckled, sometimes we just chatted about daily events. My husband had been a significant person in our lives. Being able to talk about him rather than avoiding the topic, so to speak, was so helpful.

For five weeks we never had to cook a meal because our visitors brought so many dishes of food. Often friends who brought food would stay to eat with us, cleaning up afterward, so we could go sit with the new company who inevitably would have come. Close friends came often, wanting to help with the tea and housework. I felt surrounded with care and love during those first, numbing weeks of death. I found this a healthier way to help myself as a new widow cope with death.

THE POWER OF THE MANY

I have stated before that I honestly believe it is possible to eradicate extreme poverty. One of the ways that will happen is through community. People in the developing world cannot survive without community, yet once they organize around a goal they do much more than survive. They thrive. They have shown me that the islands the rich have created must be bridged by long, abiding relationships, honest expressions of weakness and need, authentic acceptance of practical assistance, and uniting to meet the needs of others.

If we continue to live in our insulated and isolated world, we will miss the benefits that come with true community: the enduring friendships, the laughter and fun, and even the tears of those who wrap their arms around us when we grieve. Because humans are hardwired by their Creator to live in community, isolation is not an option if we are to live as whole people.

One of Jesus' clear teachings is that everyone is our neighbor. He was a master at using simple stories to convey deep truths. In the well-known parable of the good Samaritan, Jesus told of a Jewish man who had been mugged and left for dead on the side of the road. A couple of Jewish clergy passed by and went their way without getting involved. Later, a man from Samaria passed by. He not only carried the victim to safety at a nearby hotel, he arranged to pay for any care the wounded man required. Jesus then asked his audience, who knew well the generational hatred between Jews and Samaritans, "Who was the victim's neighbor?" The undeniable truth is that my neighbor is anyone and everyone, everywhere.

By celebrating this, we can be part of the revolution that will eradicate extreme poverty. We are all part of a global community, and through a variety of organizations we can help our neighbor in Ethiopia or India or Nicaragua. Let us value community and do something to help level the playing field for the other members. Let us open our hearts to others, both in the community where we are planted and in our global village. We are all stronger, and the world is a better place, when we live in community.

4

GRATITUDE

True gratitude results in generosity.

One reason why I believe we can actually eradicate poverty is the way the poor take what they are given and multiply it. While it is true that the developing world needs the initial investment that more affluent countries can provide, the seed money flows far beyond the initial recipients. Just like the story where Jesus fed five thousand people with five small loaves and a couple of fish, those in extreme poverty have a knack for multiplication, and it starts with sharing. While I truly believe that unexpected feast was a miracle, I also can imagine someone receiving a piece of bread, tearing off a portion, and being so grateful to have something to eat that he turns to the person next to him and says, "Here, have some bread."

I have seen it over and over again. Starting with a relatively small amount of money, individuals, families, and even entire villages are transformed and overcome the curse of poverty. Why? Because when someone in abject poverty receives a fair chance and succeeds, out of gratitude and compassion, he or she generously invests in others who similarly need merely a helping hand. The working poor have taught me that true gratitude results in generosity.

JUST A FEW BABY CHICKS

Perhaps the best example of how this lesson works comes from the Reverend Dr. Kwabena Darko. Darko's father died when his son was only a young boy. With the loss of the family breadwinner, young Darko combined his schooling with petty trading in order to supplement the family income. Though resources were scarce, and on many occasions the family did not know where the next meal was coming from, he did not lose hope. He continued his education part time through correspondence with the Rapid Results College in London and devoted more time to his trading activities to support the family. He later earned a scholarship to study poultry science at the Ruppin Institute in Israel. When he returned, Darko worked for his stepfather, and in five years grew their business from a flock of five thousand to one hundred thousand egg-laying chickens.

After he married, Darko started his own enterprise raising chickens with $2,000 in savings. After tithing $200 to his church, he bought nine hundred baby chicks. He still needed additional funds to pay for feed. When he approached the bank, they wouldn't allow him to enter the building because he looked like every other penniless boy who worked the local farms. Darko eventually arranged a private meeting with the sympathetic and understanding bank president, who agreed to loan him just enough money to buy feed for the chicks, using the birds as collateral.

To the surprise of everyone at the bank, including its president, Darko paid off his loan early. Naturally, they were quick to loan him more money. First he borrowed $5,000, then $100,000, and a couple years later $1,000,000, enabling him to buy more chicks and more land. The business grew, and grew fast. Within sixteen years those nine hundred birds became two hundred thousand. He built silos for grain and soon owned a fleet of several dozen trucks for transporting feed. Today he runs one of the largest chicken businesses in West Africa, and one of the most profitable private enterprises in Ghana. Darko Farms & Co., Ltd., provides most of Ghana's poultry products, including animal feed and day-old chicks to farmers. He serves on the board of directors of the central bank and was an advisor to John Kufuor when he was president of Ghana.

Out of gratitude for all God had helped him accomplish, and convinced that people are not lazy but need only a "push," Darko was determined to find a way to give back some of his blessings. In 1994 he established the equivalent of a bank for the poor and made his first loan. Darko named his nonprofit organization Sinapi Aba ("Mustard Seed") Trust, based on Jesus' teaching that faith starts out like a tiny mustard seed, but when watered and nurtured it will grow into an enormous, vibrant bush that provides shelter for many birds.

Darko's faith in the poor and his passion to bring about change in his country grew. An astute businessman, he knew the value of leverage and recruited other successful entrepreneurs and Ghanaian businesspeople who, like him, served on the board of Sinapi Aba Trust. He contributed his personal money to provide the initial loan fund for many budding entrepreneurs. He then hired an executive to manage the organization that he housed in his Darko Farms office building.

Modeling his program after the Grameen Bank in Bangladesh, he offered initial loans as low as $50. Only those whom the commercial banks considered unbankable could qualify, and the purpose of the loans was limited to starting or expanding small enterprises.

In most microfinance organizations, interest is higher than at a commercial bank, but substantially lower than what moneylenders charge—borrowers' only other alternative. Terms are typically four to six months, and the borrowers are required to meet weekly in groups of about thirty members. Because the borrowers do not provide collateral, members of the group cross-guarantee each other's loans. During the weekly meeting they make their payment of principal and interest and also receive business training to ensure their businesses succeed. If one of the members is unable to make a weekly payment, the others chip in. They know that if anyone defaults, all the others are disqualified from the next cycle of credit. Thanks to this positive peer pressure and the business training, repayment on group loans approaches 100 percent.

Darko's service to the poor took off. To keep up with the demand, he and his board aggressively raised capital in the form of donations. Over the next ten years their assets reached $7.4 million. Today, this Ghanaian nonprofit has assets of $47.7 million, and provided loans to more than 130,000 clients in 2011.

One couple who made that growth possible was Robert and Jennifer Smith, who made their first contribution to Sinapi Aba Trust in 1999. Over the next few years they added more than half a million dollars to the lending program. When the organization was growing rapidly and opening several branches in remote regions, the Smiths donated four new four-wheel drive vehicles to transport funds and loan officers to the communities where the poor lived.

They also funded a youth apprenticeship program that trained children who had been orphaned by AIDS in marketable skills such as baking, carpentry, tailoring, and welding, and placed them under the tutelage of an experienced mentor. Upon the completion of their training, the young people received loans to launch their own businesses. Many of the original graduates of this program have gone on to become mentors, teaching their trade to someone else who then received a loan and started a similar business. This program has since been replicated in several African countries where poverty and AIDS are inseparable, and where there is an escalating number of orphans as a result of the pandemic.

Like Darko, the Smiths were grateful to God for their blessings and wanted to share some of their resources in a strategic way with those who were less fortunate. They received no tangible benefit in exchange for their generosity. Rather, they derive joy from knowing they are making a significant difference in others' lives, others who will never meet them or even be able to thank them. When you are truly grateful, you become generous.

HAT TRICK

One recipient of Darko's generosity is James Kwame. James lives on his small farm with his wife and four children. He first became interested in farm animals and learned about their care while working as a clerk at a veterinarian's office. To fulfill his dream of having a farm of his own, he took on a second job as a taxi driver. About twelve years ago, with little more than $100 saved from the taxi business, he purchased one and a half acres of undeveloped land. With no access to credit and no working capital, those early years yielded little, other than what he could make from buying and selling a few goats. James's dream finally became reality in 1998 when he received his first farming loan from Sinapi Aba Trust.

Starting with an initial loan of $70, James bought some chickens and feed. Within six months he had paid off his loan. When I traveled to

Ghana and met James, he had just received a $1,700 loan, one of the largest made by Sinapi Aba Trust at the time. Our group of eight visitors sat under a large shade tree and listened to James's story and the economics of his diversified farm. Though he has only a primary school education, James keeps detailed records of his business and knows the profitability of each sector. He was most eager to tell us about the one hundred goats he is raising and the chicken coop he had just built for fifteen hundred baby chicks, adding to his three hundred mature egg layers.

James is now extending Darko's generosity. As his farm has become more productive, he has provided full-time jobs to six others in his village. Having joined James nine years ago as his first worker, Kwabena Anthony is now the farm manager. (It is customary in Ghana that children are named after the day of the week on which they were born. Kwabena means Tuesday, and all boys born on Tuesday, including Darko, receive the same first name. Kwabena will remain his name of choice; only when further clarification is needed will he be called Kwabena Anthony.)

A single man in his early twenties, Kwabena would like to marry, but for the immediate future has decided not to pursue a family. He lives on the farm with James and his family, who provide him with food and shelter. James encourages him to take time off to find a wife, but Kwabena refuses. He rarely leaves the farm. Each month, rather than taking his $30 wage in cash, he has James save the entire amount for him. He is planning to buy a piece of land of his own someday. The purchase may be delayed several years, as land has greatly increased in value since James bought his farm. Kwabena is as willing to wait for his land as he is for a wife and family. James has promised Kwabena that when the time is right, he will help him secure his own loan from Sinapi Aba Trust to establish his farm. In the meantime, if Kwabena chooses to marry, he is welcome to have his wife come to live with them on the farm.

Another gift that gave James much pleasure was donating a goat to be slaughtered for his church's Christmas celebration. Consistent with what he has read in the Bible, James was happy to be able to share what he had with those in need, in this case others in his church and community. Convinced that it is impossible to out-give God, James thought it no coincidence when the day after the festivities one of his goats gave birth to triplets.

As we were listening to his story, James's son, the youngest of his children, arrived home dressed in his orange and brown school uniform. After proudly introducing him to us, James asked the boy to go into the house and bring sodas for all the guests. While he was away, we learned that James's oldest daughter, who was twenty-one, had finished high school and was now in an advanced training program for an office position. The other two girls were still in high school. It did not escape me that at one time James had been one of the poorest of the world's poor.

The boy returned with a tray of soft drinks, a scene that I simultaneously welcomed and dreaded. Ghana is always hot, and even under the cascading shade of a dense, broad-leafed tree, we all dripped with perspiration. The mere sight of the cold drinks brought relief and refreshment. I knew, however, that this generous offering represented several days' wages for James. When I reached for my wallet to pay for the sodas, James exclaimed, "What! Do you want to rob me of my blessing?" To James, giving was a reflection of gratitude—his natural reaction to all he had received.

The hour we spent with James was an enriching experience, first walking about his farm and admiring all that had been achieved—so much with so little—and then visiting under the tree and learning from this wise man about work and life, and especially about gratitude and generosity. As we prepared to leave, James surprised us with one final gift. With a broad smile overflowing from a munificent heart, he handed us trays with three dozen freshly laid eggs.

James's parting gift was not so much the eggs as it was the message behind, and invaluable lesson that inspired, them. I'm not sure how he expected us to cook thirty-six eggs in our hotel room that night or how we might carry them on the airplane the following day. That really was not the point. Genuine gratitude is like a bird's instinctive cry. This man, rich with joy, wanted to share his blessings with others and could not resist the impulse to give.

By 1998 Sinapi Aba Trust was breaking even, covering all their operating costs from the interest and fees they charged their borrowers. Darko, however, was not satisfied. Following the evolution of microfinance, and listening to their clients, he concluded that the poor need more than credit; they need a safe place to save their money.

Commercial banks cannot make enough profit from a savings account with an opening balance of $5. So the local "*susu* collector" walks around the market every afternoon and collects small deposits from the merchants. He combines their savings and deposits them in a single bank account, but charges them a fee for his service—negative interest on their savings, if you will. Darko knew of this common practice and realized how desperate poor people are for a safe place to save what little they have.

Within a few years Darko registered an additional organization with the Ghanaian government. This new institution provided the same lending program as the other, but added the essential benefits of interest-bearing savings accounts and insurance. For the first time in their lives, these investors today have a total of more than $9 million on deposit in safe savings accounts of their own—and earn, rather than pay, interest. At the end of their workday they can make a fifty cent deposit rather than carry the extra money home and run the risk of it being consumed, or worse yet, taken and misused.

Further, instead of loaning out their own assets to the poor, the savings and loan structure is now licensed to use their loan fund as equity and borrow money against it from the World Bank and private sources. As a result, they are able to serve far more people with the same amount of money. In 2011, with minimal additional donations, the two entities loaned out more than $62 million to 191,285 of the poorest families in Ghana.

In the game of cricket, which I grew up playing, this would be a "hat trick"—three wickets taken by a bowler with three consecutive balls— similar to a single player scoring three goals in a hockey game.

First, Darko was so grateful for the help he received that he was compelled to provide affordable financial services to struggling families similar to his own.

Then, Robert and Jennifer Smith have had the joy of being a part of this dynamic organization, seeing their charitable donations used and multiplied again as businesses prosper and the loans are repaid.

Finally, James Kwame and other poor farmers have received access for the first time to capital, business training, and savings so they can know the security and dignity of caring for their families. That win-win-win forms a triangle of gratitude, like a musical triad where each of the three notes harmonizes with the others to create a beautifully complementary sound. As everyone gratefully exercises their gifts, and savings accounts are opened and more loans are made and paid back, those sound waves reverberate, touching many other lives.

GRATEFUL FOR A GRUELING LIFE

The common denominator in the stories of both Darko and James is that they began with so little. That is yet another clue about gratitude. When you aren't sure where your next meal will come from, even the smallest morsel makes you grateful. This also explains why gratitude is sometimes lacking in those of us who have so much. We take so much of our comfortable lifestyle for granted. Having a roof over our heads, food in the pantry, clothes to wear, cars to drive—even a job—all feel like things to which we are entitled. On a certain level, I am of course thankful for all I have, but I don't wake up every day exuberant over the fact that I have a closet full of clothes.

I have met people who have every reason to be bitter or resentful over what they don't have, yet exude a joyful gratitude. People like Hui Chen, who was born into a poor family in a farming community not far from the city of Hefei in eastern China. At the age of four, she was abducted and sold into slavery, one of millions of children who grow up knowing nothing but forced labor. When she was old enough, Hui was sold again as a cleaning woman and ultimately as a bride to an abusive man who over the next few years made her a mother twice. After years of suffering, she managed to escape. She went back to Hefei and never saw her two children again. There she met and subsequently worked for Wen Tsai, a kind and gentle man who operated his own small milk-delivery business. Though he was considerably younger than she, they fell in love, married, and a couple of years later had a child of their own.

Not long after Xiaoyue was born, while the struggling young family was out running errands together, their house was burglarized. They lost everything, including the bicycle used to deliver the milk. Today Hui confesses that this coda to everything else she had endured brought such grief that she began making plans to commit suicide. It was at that dark juncture, when she was about to give up all hope, that dawn broke. A friend came across a brochure advertising business loans for families like theirs. "Could this possibly be true? Would a bank loan money to an illiterate person with no collateral?" she wondered.

With nothing to lose, and buoyed by deep love for her husband and daughter, she made an inquiry. Within days Wen Tsai received a loan of $1,150 to restart his delivery business. Grateful and determined, the couple paid off the loan within six months and took out another loan, this time for $1,700. They repeated the process every six months for the next two years. Each time Wen received a slightly larger loan. Each time he expanded his enterprise. In addition to delivering milk, they used some of the profits to stock a little grocery store that Hui managed while her husband was out delivering milk. Then about three years ago, she decided to open a breakfast restaurant out of the store. She took out a loan of her own and started serving various dim sum dishes.

When I met the couple in early 2009 they were on their ninth loan, seven-year-old Xiaoyue was in second grade, they were employing two people in the restaurant and six in the milk business, and Wen had just finished reading *The One Minute Sales Person*, borrowed from his loan officer at the bank. The couple leases a second apartment where they board six of their employees, whose compensation also consists of a daily homemade breakfast, prepared for them by Hui, before they set out on their milk routes.

Exuberance and gratitude glowed in smiling eyes as this couple recounted how they had grown their enterprise and the impact they were having on their community. They made nothing of the fact that they arrive at the store every morning at 5:30 to receive and unload the *baidi*, the truck delivering dozens of racks of one-liter bottles of fresh milk. Or that by noon the six bicycles will return to the store having delivered heavy glass bottles to apartments and offices all across town. Or that at least one of the parents will remain in the store until 10:30 every evening, selling groceries while caring for their daughter. Or that this grueling routine is repeated seven days every week.

Hardship creates resilience and gratitude in a way that luxury never will. What we might consider afflictions are to the poor accomplishments, stripes of perseverance, and medals of success. Seeing her daughter gain the education she was denied brings Hui deep joy and hope. Because she was a victim herself, offering food and shelter to the homeless feeds her self-esteem. Borrowing and repaying the debt (a process she once considered impossible) creates dignity. By Western standards, the couple would still be considered poor, but for Hui Chen, who knows real slavery, hers is not a life of bondage but of bliss.

SMALL BLESSINGS HAVE HUGE REWARDS

Although I love my work, which allows me to meet and learn from people like Hui Chen, it can also be convicting. How do you respond to such gratitude in people with so little? How do you share in their happiness when their surroundings seem so appalling? I will never forget visiting a tiny tenement in one of the innumerable slums in metro Manila where I met Lola Tasun.

Lola's shelter, which she shares with five other squatters, is made of scraps of wood, tin, gunnysack, and other scavenged material. Immediately outside her front and only door is an open ditch carrying raw sewage. Running water and drains do not exist in these homes. Squatting next to the trench, she does her laundry and washes her dishes. It is there she also pours out her bath water and empties the pot after relieving herself. The open trench serves not only Lola, but also hundreds of other families in this community.

At 72, Lola should be enjoying a comfortable retirement earned through her life of hard work. But mindful that, like most others around her, if she does not work she does not eat, she works all day at a home-based microenterprise. Her venture is making simple kerosene lamps, a necessity in a community where blackouts are a common occurrence. Lola converts used glass jars into functional lamps. After painting the lid, she punches a hole in its center, through which she pokes a rope that serves as a wick. Then, from a sheet of tin, she cuts strips that she wraps around the jar, forming a secure metal handle.

Lola's lanterns sell in the immediate community for ten to twenty-five cents each, depending on the size. Two or three dollars a day is what she needs to survive. With a perpetual smile and bright twinkling eyes, she boasts that during special festivals, she hires several family members who together make as many as three hundred lamps, netting $30. I sit on the dirt floor of her home and watch as she manufactures a lamp especially for me, a gift displayed in my office to this day as a reminder to me of this remarkable woman.

And why is Lola so grateful that she would give me a lamp? She knows I am somehow connected to the world of microloans, and she has benefited from one that she has paid off on schedule. As I look at and smell Lola's surroundings, I note there is little of which to be proud and thankful. From what secret well, inside this gray-haired grandmother with only a few remaining teeth, springs such obvious and contagious exuberance? With pride and gratitude, she tells me of the loan she received and repaid with interest. This loan was no scam from the local loan shark, but a legitimate transaction from a nongovernmental organization helping her along the road to prosperity.

How could a $50 loan have given this impoverished woman so much to be thankful for? What could previously have been any worse than the surroundings she endures now? My every sense is mortified by the filth, repugnant odors, lack of privacy, discomfort, danger, ugliness, lack of sanitation, and constant noise that Lola contends with daily. How could that $50 dollar loan have changed her life so that she is now overflowing with gratitude?

Prior to receiving the loan, Lola would spend the first part of every day scavenging other people's garbage to gather enough jars for the day's production of lamps. Then for several hours, she would squat in front of her house and clean them, flushing any remaining food or grime into the shallow trench where it would merge with other garbage, bathing water, human feces, and the occasional toy lost by a child playing upstream. Finally, after scrubbing the jars and lids, soaking them in murky water, scraping off the labels, and drying them, Lola was ready to begin making the kerosene lanterns. In the remaining hours of the day, she would try to make and sell enough lamps to buy her evening meal so she would not go to bed hungry.

With the new capital from her small loan, Lola arranged with the recycling company to regularly deliver to her doorstep enough spotless jars for her daily manufacturing. She now begins each day with the grunt work behind her. She has more time to dedicate to the less demanding part of the process, which she enjoys: making and selling the lamps.

Lola still lives in a tiny shed with five other people. She still contends with raw sewage running in front of her home. But she doesn't have to work as hard as she once did, and now she has hope. For the first time in her life, she is turning a profit and has started saving. She could have sold that lamp she gave me and added to her income, but gratitude trumped profit that day.

As I rise to leave, I bend over—in part because the roof of her little hovel is too low for me to stand erect—and hug Lola. I have nothing but thanks and admiration for what this grateful woman has taught me. Lola's loan, a few dollars of savings, and a lighter burden each morning has made the poverty around her a bit more bearable

Seeing her thankfulness, despite having so little, has made me more grateful for things I so often take for granted, not one of which Lola will ever experience. In my case that list includes a two-story, single-family home with eight-foot ceilings, running water, and three flushing toilets; dependable electricity and garbage service; green lawns and paved streets; two cars and a garage; health care and life insurance; a full set of teeth and dental service should that change; college education for my children; vacations and opportunities for renewal and self-actualization; a checking account and a retirement fund; credit cards and a house mortgage; three nutritious meals a day; and a host of other contrasting luxuries.

WHAT KEEPS US FROM BEING GRATEFUL?

When I meet people like Lola, I often find myself whispering a prayer: *Lord, teach me to be grateful.* It is a sincere prayer because when you see the level of gratitude among the world's poorest, it's contagious. But to reach that goal—to become the kind of person who is truly thankful for even the smallest blessings in life—you have to make room in your heart for gratitude, and that may be as foreign for you as it was for me.

On one trip to Asia, I woke up in the middle of the night feeling prompted to pray. Concluding it was jet lag that would not allow me to sleep, I decided that rather than fight the insomnia I would spend the next couple of hours talking to God. I asked his Spirit to open my eyes that I might see whatever lesson he had for me. I invited him to shine his spiritual spotlight on my innermost being and identify anything that was displeasing to him. I recited back to him in prayer something I had memorized many years ago from Psalm 139:

> Search me, God, and know my heart;
> test me and know my anxious thoughts.
> See if there is any offensive way in me.

If you've ever heard the phrase, "Be careful what you pray for," there's a lot of truth in it. God took me at my word and opened my eyes to an inner sewer far more wretched than the gully in front of Lola's house. God lovingly answered my prayer and showed me something I really did not want to admit to or deal with. His Holy Spirit enabled me to recognize that at the root of much of what I did and aspired to, there was nothing other than pride. I wrestled in bed, at times turning my head to the side, as if trying to look away. What I saw was disgusting. I strive to raise money for the poor so my colleagues will admire me. I yearn to be spiritual so my wife and family will respect me. I want to speak at conferences so my mug shot will appear in a glossy brochure.

What could be more abhorrent than to want very good things for bad reasons? The more I evaluated my true motives, the more defiled I felt. For more than an hour, as I prayed, God convicted me of this horrendous pride. I wouldn't wish this awful revelation on anyone, nor would I trade this spiritual confrontation for any other emotional high. In the midst of this encounter came the soothing message that I had been forgiven. The existence of my pride was no revelation to my loving Father, who knows everything about each of us. God sees our actions and also sees into our hearts. We can hide nothing from his scrutiny.

The only thing that changed on this particular night was my own awareness of my pride. God took no pleasure in rubbing my nose in it. On the contrary, once I acknowledged the gravity of my condition, he not only reassured me of his unending love for me, but showed me how to overcome my pride. After about two hours of struggling and praying, I sensed God's Spirit revealing to me the true antidote to pride. Gratitude. How can I be proud of something that is not my doing; something for which I can take no credit; something for which I am deeply grateful?

Conversely, how can I be truly grateful for something I feel I have accomplished on my own; something to which I am entitled; something of which I am proud? Pride and gratitude are mutually exclusive.

Pride is rooted in my own neediness. It causes me to take rather than give. It allows me to criticize and judge others. It prevents me from loving my neighbor. It keeps me from acknowledging God's many blessings. It is at the root of so much that is destructive: greed, deceit, lust, covetousness, gossip, unfaithfulness, disrespect, revenge, selfishness.

My understanding of gratitude has been transformed by the poorest people in the world. Despite poverty and difficult lives, these people seemed truly grateful, and I wanted desperately to share that same thankful spirit. In our materialistic culture, we are taught that happiness and thankfulness flow from bounty. Advertisers would have us believe the bumper sticker, "He who dies with the most toys wins." Since infancy, everyone from parents to Santa Claus has instilled in us the idea that if we are good, we get. Hollywood's recurring theme is that fame and riches bring joy and fulfillment. We know it isn't true, but we live as if it is. And along the way we begin to believe that all the blessings we enjoy come from our own cleverness or ability.

A perfect breeding ground for pride.

It took a long and mostly dreadful night to recognize that I would never enjoy the grateful spirit I witnessed in so many unexpected places around the world as long as I held on to my pride. Poverty is frequently the bedfellow of inexplicable gratitude. With all my richness, I had not truly experienced it. On that dark night, God showed me my inner poverty. He replaced the emptiness of my pride with the gift of joy and gratitude.

5

PERSISTENCE

Hardship creates persistence in a way that luxury does not.

One blessing of living in an affluent country is that we get what we want and need, and we often get it fairly quickly. Think about it. If you want a new pair of jeans, you go to a store and buy them. Whether it's designer or resale-shop jeans, we have almost unlimited access and choice. Or let's say it's the middle of winter in the Midwest and you feel like eating an orange. Although you may have to drive through the snow, you can walk into virtually any grocery store and buy an orange harvested in Florida just a few days earlier. Thanks to relatively easy credit, most of us don't have to save up before we make a major purchase. From computers to washing machines, our purchases are just a card-swipe away.

In the developing world, life moves a lot more slowly. For example, something as simple as getting a drink of water is a complex and intense process in many countries. First, someone has to walk to a stream, which may be several miles away. Then she fills a container from the stream and balances all thirty pounds of it (or more) on her head for the long walk home. Returning to her village, she builds a fire from wood she gathered earlier in the day, pours a few quarts of water into a metal pot, and waits for it to boil. Only after the water has boiled and cooled is it ready to drink. For the majority of the world's poor, clean running water at the turn of a faucet in their homes does not exist. And so they persist.

Day after day, they make the long trek to the stream. They scavenge through someone's garbage. They bend over to plant seeds in the hot sun. They put up with the challenges of being at the lowest position in the socioeconomic landscape. When I am working on a difficult project and feel as if I can't stand to spend another minute on it, I think of the remarkable persistence of the working poor. It causes me to dive right back in.

THE BIRTH OF THE "CORPORATIVE"

In my work in international development, I like to see results. When bureaucracy or corruption or just human inefficiency gets in the way, I can become impatient. That's when I put into practice what I have learned from those living in developing regions—people like Father Benigno P. Beltran.

For twenty-five years, this Roman Catholic priest worked with scavengers who lived on and around the infamous Smokey Mountain garbage dump in Manila. Father Ben, as he is affectionately known, launched his own microenterprise development program for many of the residents in the area. His ministry to the poor is far more comprehensive than anything else I've seen.

In many microfinance organizations, almost all entrepreneurs repay their loans at the rate of 95 percent or more. Whereas repayment is extremely high, so is renewal. After their first small loan of $50, most loan recipients remain dependent on credit, borrowing again and again. They could not survive, and certainly could not grow their enterprises, without continued access to borrowing. It is not uncommon for them to take out five or ten consecutive loans over a period of years, each with a four- to six-month term and each slightly larger than the previous one. In all microenterprise programs, only a few of the borrowers create a mid-sized business, employ significant numbers of workers, and no longer require credit. This should not surprise us, as it is not unlike the way most of us in the West perpetually borrow against future income.

Father Ben's premise is that, even with consecutive microloans, the people at the bottom of the world's economic food chain are too vulnerable to compete alone in the marketplace. Rather than individually making or selling identical widgets and pitting themselves against each other, under his tutelage they band together into an empowered community that carries force in the market. Father Ben argues that in the status quo, the middlemen who have the capital make most of the profit, while the poor who buy and sell do most of the work.

Growing and selling rice in the Philippines is a classic example. Destitute peasants toil under the equatorial sun to plant and harvest rice. These farmers live three to twelve hours from Manila, the market with the highest demand. Wealthy middlemen create a monopoly by providing the only transportation to market and the only outlet for the farmers' produce. The middlemen pay the farmers a small fraction of what they will sell it for, pocketing the balance and leaving the hardworking farmers impoverished.

On the other end, the poor retailers in Manila have no option but to pay the middlemen multiple times what was paid to the farmers. The retailers have no way of knowing the farmers' selling price, let alone having direct access to the produce. The inflated cost leaves the retailers barely able to survive off of their small markup. In addition to the farmer and retailer remaining poor, people from the poor communities who ultimately buy the rice are also affected by the higher prices. Father Ben is persuaded that it is primarily the unethical and unscrupulous middlemen, plus corruption at many points along the chain, including the police and market authorities, that keep the poor in bondage.

His strategy is to create a cooperative that needs only the growers and sellers. In this scenario, the farmers are paid substantially more for their produce and the retailers are charged far less. In addition to enabling them both to make more profit, the rice also sells for considerably less to the end users living around Smokey Mountain. A very small portion of the recovered profits are retained by the co-op to cover the cost of its operations.

What makes this model unique among the poor, and indeed even possible, is the introduction of modern technology. Using refurbished computers, the retailers selling the rice in Manila control their inventory by buying only what they have pre-sold. They visit each member in their community, taking orders from each family. The retailer's request travels electronically to hundreds of farmers living in the surrounding rural areas, who are also members of the co-op. The farmers communicate with each other electronically and in turn ship only the amount that the retailers have sold.

Conversely, the farmers place orders with the co-op members in the city for the merchandise they want from the city. They submit the order for merchandise via the Internet to the co-op center in Manila, where it is filled primarily by the microenterprises of fellow co-op members. When the truck leaves the city, it is filled with the vegetables, sardines, shoes, and other commodities included on the electronic list of merchandise. Bank checks made possible by the cooperative, rather than currency, complete the transactions.

The cooperative leases trucks as needed. Eventually they intend to purchase their own. Either way, the co-op members save on transportation costs because the trucks travel to the city loaded with rice and return to the rural areas filled with products the farmers ordered. Co-op members also avoid any markup on the transportation because their own members drive and handle the shipments. They also eliminate loss stemming from corruption as they are the only ones with access to the produce. Because of this, they avoid paying bribes and other illegitimate surcharges along the way. One of Father Ben's innovative strategies includes assigning a priest to accompany each of the trucks. He hopes the priest's presence will appeal to the decency and morality of the police and others who might otherwise be tempted to extort or take further advantage of the poor.

The initial pilot program comprised three thousand families, including some from the twenty-five thousand residents that used to live on the Smokey Mountain garbage dump. Farmers and others in the rural communities have also chosen to participate. When I visited Father Ben, he had mobilized some 850 people in the area immediately surrounding Smokey Mountain.

What I find so amazing about Father Ben's co-op is that it did not emerge overnight or even in a few years. The dream was born twenty years ago and faced seemingly insurmountable barriers every step of the way. He never gave up, but faced each obstacle with resolve and creativity. Knowing the importance of having political allies to realize his dream, during the 1992 Phillipine presidential election he marshaled a voting block of fifty thousand poor people and sought to arrange a visit to Smokey Mountain by each of the candidates. Fidel V. Ramos was the only one to accept the invitation. With Father Ben's backing, Ramos became president of the Philippines. On October 8, 1992, on his one-hundredth day in office, and true to his pledge to the residents of the dump, President Ramos inaugurated the Smokey Mountain Development and Reclamation Project.

Following that announcement, the government removed much of the garbage and in its place constructed several four-story apartment buildings for the former residents. A large two-story complex also housed the co-op's staging area, warehouse, market stalls, offices, religious training facility, computer training center, and Internet server. Father Ben received a donation of five hundred refurbished computers from a church in Portland, Oregon. He then arranged for a team of a dozen college and post-graduate students through InterVarsity Christian Fellowship. These volunteers, some of them MBA students at Harvard, spent the summer in Manila helping design the computer systems and implementing strategies. When I was with him, Father Ben was preparing thirty young people from the Philippines to travel to the United States to study entrepreneurial management.

As technology progressed further, the poor responded quickly. Today many rural farmers use cell phones and text messaging to advertise their crops to buyers in the cities. No longer hostage to only one buyer, these farmers shop around, take multiple offers, find out what other farmers are asking, negotiate prices, arrange deliveries, and even check the weather forecast and research crop insurance, all from a cell phone.

Father Ben refers to this new infrastructure as a "corporative." It combines the best features of a corporation in terms of management structure, competition, incentives, and research and development with the heart of a cooperative, in that it is people-centered and exists to serve its members. Without the persistence of Father Ben and many who worked with him, rice farmers and merchants would still be at the mercy of the harsh system that once kept them in poverty.

THE LONG VIEW

One of the ways the poor demonstrate their perseverance is in their willingness to do what must be done, including separation from family, to pursue an education or better work. For those fortunate few poor students who receive scholarships to study abroad, it is not unusual to be separated from family for as many as six years. This is especially true for African students. The scholarship covers their school expenses, but they cannot afford trips home between semesters or during the summer. Their commitment to education wins out over homesickness because they know they are on a path out of poverty.

It is common in the Philippines, where wages are low, unemployment high, and prices comparable to those in the U.S., for one parent to live abroad and send money home to the family. Increasingly, these transfers of money create a stable source of family income, particularly for parents who have no college degree. Remittances, as they are called, now head the list of factors building the Philippine economy. This influx of cash is greater than the yield from agriculture, manufacturing, tourism, or any other source. No other country in the world has its economy flooded by as much money from citizens living outside its borders. Despite the strain this separation places on marriages and families, many make the necessary sacrifice for months or even years at a stretch.

On a trip to Manila I hired a man named Reynard to drive me across the city, and the ever-present gridlock gave the two of us the opportunity for a lengthy talk. Reynard's story gave me a fresh awareness of the strain placed on families when poverty necessitates lengthy separations. During most of their married lives, Reynard and his wife, Chara, have lived apart. They have two children. With three years of college education as an architect, but a little short of a degree, Reynard has never managed to find a job in his field, or any constant work for that matter. Shortly after he and Chara married, he secured a contract in Korea as a master cutter for a garment factory, making men's clothing. When the two-year contract expired, he came home. Still unable to find a job in the Philippines, he signed another contract in Taiwan, this time in a watch-manufacturing plant where he spray-painted and baked the faces on wristwatches. Over the following three years, Reynard came home only once for a brief vacation.

Next he found work in Japan, this time for five years. Salaries there soared in comparison, but so did the cost of living. Fortunately, he obtained free board in a loft above the manufacturing plant where he ran a machine that made various vinyl products. His employer also provided most of his meals, so every month for five years, Reynard sent virtually his entire paycheck to his wife in the Philippines.

By the time he returned home, Chara had departed to work in Hong Kong as a domestic helper, leaving their daughter, Maricon, with Reynard's parents. Chara's family lived as peasant farmers about 150 miles from Manila, where they cultivated rice by hand. Their dire poverty had forced Chara to drop out of college after one year, making regular employment in the Philippines as likely as a meal without rice. This time, Reynard and Chara didn't see each other for more than four years, communicating primarily by email and weekend phone calls.

On one of Reynard's visits to Hong Kong, Chara became pregnant and had to come home to deliver their son. The money that Reynard had saved during the years in Japan enabled them to buy a small piece of land in the country near Chara's parents. They dreamed of building their own home. In the meantime, the family of four moved in with Reynard's parents. His younger sister, educated and fluent in English, moved to America under an assignment with the Philippines embassy. Reynard took over the payments on her SUV and ran the equivalent of a limousine or taxi service. That is how I met him.

Reynard acknowledged that being separated from his family was difficult, especially when it came to his relationship with his children. But it was the only way their family could enjoy a slightly better standard of living than their destitute neighbors. He hopes he will be able to help his children obtain the education he was never able to finish. "I work for my babies," he says.

Even with my extensive travel schedule, Lise and I have never been apart for more than three weeks at a time. I cannot imagine being away from her for any longer, let alone a year or more. Yet for Reynard and others like him, there is simply no other choice. In the face of emotionally draining circumstances, the hardworking poor persevere for the sake of their loved ones. I have much to learn from them about what is essential and eternal. But this heartbreaking lifestyle—and the hardship it inflicts on every family member—should not be their only option for survival. Their selfless commitment inspires me to do whatever I can to provide new and better financial opportunities for families like Reynard's, enabling them to build a life together, rather than apart.

ENTREPRENEUR OF THE YEAR

Perhaps the most amazing example of how the poor persevere begins in a small rural town in Zimbabwe. A little girl named Theresa Nkosi was forced to drop out of school to help her mother make and sell brooms from grass and sticks they cut themselves. In so many developing countries this story is repeated. If the choice is between survival and an education, it really isn't a choice. Theresa could not go to school.

Like many African girls, Theresa was married as a teenager and soon began raising children of her own. In her early thirties she followed her husband to the capital city, where he hoped to find work. Shortly after they settled in Harare, Theresa's husband deserted her and their four children, leaving her even poorer. Determined to keep her children in school, she became a domestic maid for *three* families. For many years this resolute woman worked twelve to fourteen hours every day, washing laundry by hand, cooking, cleaning, ironing, caring for children, and providing whatever service the white families needed before returning home to her own children.

Clearly, the driving force behind her self-discipline was her commitment to provide her children with the education she'd never received. They, too, learned early on what it meant to work hard and long. Every morning their mother woke them at three o'clock so that before school they could wash the dishes, clean the house, and supplement their mother's income by selling eggs, tomatoes, onions, and other vegetables. Then after school, while their mother was still at work, the children did the shopping and prepared dinner.

Theresa eventually remarried and gave birth to a fifth child, which provided the impetus to earn a living while staying at home. Inspired by her children's successful vegetable-selling efforts, she obtained a small loan and opened a little vegetable store at the front of her house.

With strong will and determination, women like Dorcas, shown in her sorghum
fields in Kenya, are helping to create a better world for the next generation.

Top: The rickshaw operator in India who helped me understand that poverty and luxury are products of our birthplace (see page 27).

Above: My dear friends Jacque and John, whose commitment to the poor exemplifies their desire to live as Jesus did (see page 165).

Above: An example of the resourceful creativity of many impoverished entrepreneurs, Lola proudly displays the lamp she made as a gift for me (see page 84).

Above: Women like Menika and the group of entrepreneurs she leads have shown me the power of community (see page 66).

Left: Menika demonstrates the wet-grinder that equipped her to care for her family of eight (see page 68).

Below: Esther (left) and her sister, both HIV-positive, hope to maintain their farm and train their children to eventually tend it on their own (see page 38).

Poverty leads many children around the world to take desperate measures simply to survive—including working in dangerous or harmful conditions.

Jon Warren/World Vision, 2004

Like the ragpickers I met in India, these children in Cambodia sort through trash to earn a living (see page 127).

This young girl from Guatemala reminds me of the girl who tried
to sell me potholders (see page 132).

Mauricio Rosaldo/World Vision, 2008

Jon Warren/World Vision, 2008

Top: Setiawan with the chickens that help him feed his carp, which swim under the coop. This creative system provides him with both fish and eggs to sell (see page 141).

Center: Raising and selling fish helped this man and others in his region of Mexico to revive their local economy after severe flooding.

Above: Running a small fish and vegetable stand provides this HIV-positive Zambian woman with income.

*The work ethic and creativity demonstrated by people in the
developing world prove that poverty is not simply a result of
laziness or lack of ability.*

Jon Warren/World Vision, 2009

Top: These industrious women participate in a group project, carrying bricks that will be marketed to builders.

Above: Theresa gives me hope for a world without extreme poverty. Despite having only a third-grade education, this creative entrepreneur owns several successful businesses, including one selling homemade popsicles to the children pictured with her here (see page 96).

Left: My older brother and me leaving New York for South Africa on a freighter in 1955 (see page 31).

Below left: My siblings and I have fond memories of growing up in South Africa. I'm on the far right, and in the pot is Randy, who died of cancer 40 years later (see page 71).

Top: By partnering with other farmers in his community, Yohana moved from smallholder farming to commercial farming, dramatically increasing his profits (see page 176).

Above: Three of every four people in sub-Saharan Africa depend on agriculture for their livelihoods. Moses and his wife, Betty, grow coffee, mangoes, bananas, and more.

Jon Warren/World Vision, 2009

Jon Warren/World Vision, 2010

Above: Like the women I met in Kenya once did (see page 181), millions of mothers and children around the world still walk miles daily to get water—a time-consuming task that competes with more productive activities. In this Ethiopian village, people often wait in long lines (after walking over hot, dry terrain) to fill their jerry cans with water that's contaminated.

Left: Improved access to water makes all the difference for families and farmers who need a reliable means of irrigating their fields. Here, community members in Kenya work together to replace a ruptured pipeline that provides them with clean water.

Microloans equip hardworking entrepreneurs around the world to start a wide variety of manufacturing businesses …

Jon Warren/World Vision, 2009

Jon Warren, World Vision, 2000

Katia Maldonado/World Vision, 2006

Jon Warren, World Vision, 2008

Top left: Producing roofing tiles in Rwanda

Above left: Furniture making in El Salvador

Top right: Basket weaving in Myanmar

Above right: Embroidery in Mexico

Jon Warren/World Vision, 2002

Gina Castellanos/World Vision, 2011

Top: Entrepreneurs like this woman from Peru open small stores selling produce and other goods on the side of the road or in open-air markets.

Above: Thanks to small loans and training, Marianela and her family have increased their harvests and started a business selling produce from their home in Honduras.

*Microloans help hardworking women use existing
skills to generate income ...*

Jon Warren/World Vision, 2010

Jeanice Vargas/World Vision, 2008

Jon Warren/World Vision, 2008

Above: This kitchen belongs to a restaurant opened by ten women in El Salvador with the help of a microloan.

Top: Every day, Gloria bakes more than 500 pounds of bread to sell in her Bolivian community.

Above: Mao Chea, who grows rice in Cambodia, received small loans that provided her family with the means to increase their income. Her fields remind me of the rice paddies I saw in Yohana's community in Tanzania (see page 176).

Abby Metty/World Vision, 2010

Wenda Paipi/World Vision, 2011

Top: With the help of a loan and training, this family from Honduras started a plantain farm that provides the financial resources they need to keep their children in school.

Above: Mildy Susu of Zambia cares for eight children of his own, as well as two orphans. Microloans empowered him to improve his harvests and enabled him to send all ten children to school.

*Learning new skills gives motivated people
the tools they need to succeed ...*

Top: At a shelter for women in the Democratic Republic of the Congo, training in skills such as basket weaving and other handcrafts gives those affected by conflict a new start in life.

Above: A sewing group in Tanzania provides young mothers with new skills to help them support their families.

Jon Warren/World Vision, 2008

Abby Metty/World Vision, 2010

Top: Thanks to his carpentry business, Crisanto (middle) is able to stay in Mexico—rather than leave the country in search of work—and provide for his ten children.

Above: Celestina's *rosquillas* factory enables her to provide for her family and creates jobs that benefit her Honduran community.

Over time her inventory expanded to include other perishables, soda, candy, and a variety of items we're accustomed to finding at our local mini-marts. While the store was no larger than a typical refreshment stand at a little-league baseball game, she proudly referred to it as a supermarket.

Soon Theresa opened a second supermarket across town and hired a manager. A year or so later she took out a second loan, this time to buy firewood. She arranged for truckloads of logs to be delivered regularly and dumped near her store. Then she employed someone to cut, stack, and sell firewood to people living in the neighborhood, all of whom rely on wood-burning stoves for their cooking and to boil drinking water.

In short order she paid off the firewood loan and took out a third loan, still less than $1,000, to buy a commercial-grade hairdryer and basic hairdressing supplies. Again she hired a woman from the neighborhood, someone who knew how to cut hair. Theresa converted one of the rooms of her small house into a beauty salon. In no time, she saved enough money to furnish a second chair, and then a third. She bought more equipment and hired more women to keep up with the demand. I can still picture the three women, dressed in their matching pink and white uniforms, all busily working on different customers' hair, and Theresa looking on with the pride of a coach after her team had just pulled off a major upset. At night, she reclaimed the hair salon as sleeping quarters for her family.

With a fourth loan, Theresa added on to the side of her house and used the space as a game room for children in her community. She bought a used foosball table and a couple of outdated arcade games. This safe and wholesome place offered peace of mind to the parents in the neighborhood. They knew their children would play under the watchful eye of their friend, whom they called Ambuya Nkosi. (*Ambuya* means *grandma* in the Shona language.)

Once she paid off that investment, this entrepreneur with a third-grade education borrowed money to buy a freezer. Every evening she would partially fill small plastic baggies with different flavored fruit drinks. She would seal the bags by melting the open end over a candle. Then she placed the sealed baggies in the freezer. The following day she sold the sweet popsicles for a few cents to the children walking home after a hot day of classes. The afternoon I visited Theresa, about thirty small children milled around this convenient stop-off point, a house that a couple of years ago had been merely her simple convenience store.

Now in her eighties, Theresa begins her workday at four in the morning with the bookkeeping for her four businesses. At seven o'clock she starts her rounds, inspecting the different operations. She still runs the firewood stand and the supermarkets, although she closed the beauty salon when her husband, who has since died, became bedridden. Recently, she added another business: she is the distributor for Coca-Cola in her area. She sells soda by the case to others who then sell bottles from their homes or on the street. She also sold the video games to make room for a funeral business, selling caskets and related items. The last I heard, she was applying for a loan to buy a truck, one that could both be used as a delivery vehicle for the wholesale soda business and function as a hearse. With AIDS devastating her nation, and life expectancy in the thirties at that time (two of her sons died at a young age), the demand for her latest enterprise was on the rise.

In 2004, a television interviewer asked Theresa the secret to her success. She replied, "I give the credit to my mother, who taught and encouraged me to work hard and fear God." She said her mother told her that because of her poverty, belief in God was the only inheritance she could leave her. Today Theresa passes on this spiritual encouragement to her fifteen grandchildren and two great-grandchildren, praying for each one every day.

While Theresa's story is extraordinary, I am continually amazed at the way the poor persevere in the face of repeated hurdles and setbacks. This quality reinforces my conviction that we will see poverty eradicated. It will not be easy. It wasn't easy for Reynard to be separated from his family for years at a time. Father Ben could have given up on his dream to create a more equitable rice market and stuck to his work inside his church's doors. Theresa could have given up when her first husband left—and no one would have blamed her.

I'm thankful I live in a country where I can get pretty much anything I need immediately. But the possibility of near-instant gratification sometimes has a darker side. Life is full of setbacks and surprises, some momentous, that must be overcome. In a land of plenty, we resent that fact and expect life to follow a comfortable and secure path. This mentality shows up in little ways—becoming impatient when the meal we order is slow to arrive at the table, or showing disgust when the repair shop can't get to our job for another week. It's damaging in even more significant ways when we give in to repeated temptations or walk away from difficult relationships. The working poor have taught me that compared to the delays and inconveniences they endure, my problems are small. Surely I can wait patiently another minute while the minimum-wage restaurant cook prepares my meal. I can accept a temporary setback at work. I can commit to persevering through the challenges of maintaining healthy relationships. I can continue to work hard and have faith for the future even after I'm downsized by my company as a result of the difficult economy.

When I reflect on inspiring stories of persistence like Reynard's and Theresa's, and begin to imagine a world without extreme poverty, I get excited. I remember the apostle Paul's exhortation in Galatians 6:9, "Let us not become weary in doing good, for at the proper time we will reap a harvest if we do not give up."

Let's not give up. Together we can help end extreme poverty.

6

SELF-RELIANCE

The working poor long to break free from the

chains of poverty and become fully self-reliant.

Try to imagine yourself as a Haitian parent with a spouse and two children. Because you were born in Haiti instead of the U.S., it's been a struggle since the day you were born to find enough food to eat, clothes to wear, a place to sleep at night. As a child, you went to a little school run by Catholic nuns, but had to drop out when your parents could no longer afford the meager fees. On the days when your father couldn't find work, you went to the church for your one meal of the day. You were thankful for the food, but you felt a little embarrassed to be eating there instead of in your home. Because you had no older siblings, when you grew out of your clothes, your mom took you to another church run by white missionaries who gave you a pair of pants and a shirt that fit. Something about the way the missionaries patted you on the head made you grateful and angry at the same time.

By the time you were eighteen, you had married but were still living in your parents' home, hoping to eventually be able to afford your own place. Like your parents, you show up every morning at a vacant lot where contractors and farmers hire day laborers, but most days there isn't any work. In a hand-to-mouth economy, no work means no money. Thankfully, there are numerous relief organizations where you can get free rice for the day's meal. But there's something about standing in that rice line that rips a bit of soul out of you. You appreciate the kindness of these strangers, but the very act of reaching for that little bag of rice is a blatant reminder that you can't put food on the table for yourself. Every time you accept a handout, you exchange a portion of your dignity and self-esteem for the rice.

Some days, after standing in the hot sun for hours waiting for someone to hire you, you walk to the harbor, look out over the bay, and dream of being able to tell your spouse: "I got a good job today! It pays enough for us to rent our own apartment. Now we won't have to stand in line for free rice or go to the church for our clothes. Maybe every once in a while we'll even be able to go to that little café around the corner and have someone bring us our meal!"

One of the most profound lessons I have learned from the poor is this: they do not want to live off of handouts. They are thankful for the generosity from developed nations. They know the gifts from afar are often necessary, but what they *really* want is to take care of themselves. Not to depend on others, but to be self-reliant.

Why isn't that the first thing that comes to mind when discussing this issue? The poor most of us see are the panhandlers and homeless in our cities. At the risk of making an unfair generalization, the people who approach you in the city for a handout have hit bottom. At one point in their misfortune they most likely did everything they could to find work, but failed for any number of reasons that might have included lack of skill or education, addiction, or disability. They quickly spiraled into the depths of poverty.

So when we think of the poor, we often think of a disheveled individual begging for money to feed their addictions. Perhaps with pity and compassion, perhaps feeling a little indignant, we walk quickly past the outstretched hand. Sadly, this situation exists all over the world, but from my experience and observations, people in this condition have little in common with the millions of hardworking poor in the developing world. The vast majority of the poor I have met through the years are people with great dignity and pride. While they did not choose to live under such difficult conditions, they face each day with great courage. They love their families just as we love ours. They have dreams and aspirations, and are somehow able to hold onto slivers of hope in the direst of circumstances. From Afghanistan to Zimbabwe, the majority of those we call "poor" have an innate drive to live successfully without depending on anyone else for their well-being.

GOOD DEEDS, QUESTIONABLE RESULTS

A good friend once visited Honduras and asked a priest what message he could take back to people in the United States. The priest's response was initially quite startling: "Please tell your American contacts not to be so generous."

Naturally my friend was not expecting that reply. He probed a little deeper. The priest explained to him that periodically parishes and churches in America collect their used clothing and, in the name of charity, send off huge shipments to villages in Honduras. The poor of the community are the recipients of the shoes and clothing. That is just about everyone.

Within weeks, every seamstress, tailor, shoemaker, and storeowner selling clothing in town is out of business. Then, with no market for their clothing, they have no income to buy other people's products. A downward cycle begins, and soon the fragile economy of the little village is hemorrhaging. Those self-reliant few have, in the name of charity, been made dependent.

The destructive nature of co-dependency is not limited to rural villages in Honduras, but also applies to inter-country charitable donations. Bolivia has been among the poorest nations in the Western hemisphere for many years, with Honduras, Nicaragua, and Haiti being the only countries with a lower GDP. Why does a nation as large as Texas and Arkansas combined, with a population of less than ten million people, need to import eggs, particularly when 40 percent of its population is involved in agriculture? Part of the answer is a little-known tragedy a few decades back that robbed the masses of their self-reliance.

In the early '80s, government-subsidized farmers in the U.S. produced far more wheat than they could possibly consume or sell. The solution to the U.S. problem was to donate shiploads of wheat to impoverished Bolivia. The overabundance of free wheat had an effect similar to the one created by the donations of used clothing in Honduras. Suddenly, with free wheat available, Bolivian grain farmers had no market for their produce. Even those growing barley and corn had to contend with the fact that former customers were substituting wheat in their diet.

I visited Bolivia about that time. Thousands of small farmers, no longer able to make a living off of their grain, were planting coca leaves—a much more lucrative cash crop. In the years that followed, the U.S. paid dearly for its ill-conceived "generosity," experiencing a huge influx of illegal cocaine from Bolivia as well as Colombia and other South American countries.

If I have learned anything in my career in international development, it's that when it comes to helping the poor, one size doesn't fit all. One reason I am so confident that we will eradicate poverty is that we really do have enough resources to get the job done. Again and again, ordinary citizens, corporations, and governments in the developed world have demonstrated their generosity in ways that convince me that lack of money is not the primary problem. Knowing precisely how to deploy resources—relief and development—is crucial to the battle.

RELIEF AND DEVELOPMENT

Obviously there are times of crisis or disaster when survival, rather than self-reliance, is the objective. Consider the 2010 earthquake in Haiti. Immediately after much of Port-au-Prince collapsed, the millions who lost everything did not need a small loan to start a business. They needed water, food, medicine, and shelter. The outpouring from around the world was staggering—it came so fast and in such quantities that workers on the ground could barely keep up with it. With an already fragile economy shattered, and the region's infrastructure virtually destroyed, the people in and around Port-au-Prince will most likely need this type of aid for years to come.

Because of tragedies we can neither predict nor control—famine, drought, earthquakes, civil war—we will always need to provide emergency relief, and we should all be thankful for nonprofit organizations that respond promptly and strategically to such disastrous calamities. But we also need to expand our own thinking about how best to provide ongoing help to the poor.

Typically, the images of suffering we see on the evening news after a major tragedy move us instantly to action. For example, there was a tremendous outpouring of charity in the days following the Indian Ocean tsunami that devastated a dozen countries on December 26, 2004. As in Haiti, massive amounts of aid were donated within hours to provide the survivors with the bare necessities to stay alive. Americans and other citizens in the developed world always respond generously when disaster strikes. But when the television cameras and news crews leave, the need shifts from relief to a more sustainable type of assistance.

Without minimizing the impact of that tsunami, the 250,000 lives suddenly swept away is equal to the number of children under five years of age who currently die from preventable causes *every thirteen days*. Obviously, we need to respond to crises as generously as possible, but what do we do about the equally devastating problem of chronic hunger and disease?

It is estimated that nearly 800 children die *every hour* from causes that could be prevented. That means that today, and every day, nearly 19,000 children will quietly slip from life as undetected and irretrievable as the colorful leaves of autumn dropping from the trees. This silent calamity will happen every day of the coming year, and no one other than their families and friends will take note. The gross tragedy of it all is that the vast majority of these deaths are not due to a lack of global resources. Other than in times of crisis, in most countries where the poor live, there is plenty of food to go around. Millions of parents of children with bellies distended by malnourishment walk past huge markets of fresh and nutritious food every day. And worldwide, there are plenty of vaccines available, plenty of bed nets. The issue is that the poor simply do not have the money to buy the food and medicine they need to keep their children healthy.

The long-term solution to this unbelievable situation is not relief, but development. Give a hand up, not a handout. Give a knitting machine, not a sweater. Relief responds to the immediate emergency. Development provides long-term, self-sustaining solutions by addressing the root of systemic problems. Relief may allow someone to survive today, but it will never empower that person to become self-reliant tomorrow. Obviously both are needed, but before we rush in with emergency relief, we need to make sure it's the right course of action. As my friend saw in Honduras, handouts can destroy.

LISTENING TO THE POOR

In 1991, southern Africa was facing the worst drought of the twentieth century, and Zimbabwe, the region's breadbasket, was unable to feed its own people. There is a fertile rural area near Harare called the Domboshawa Valley that was home to several thousand small farms. The people were hungry. No one wants to see children starve, so the temptation was to begin shipping in tons of food to help people ride out the crisis. On the surface, a massive relief effort made sense, because once the drought had passed, people could return to their livelihood—farming.

However, the farmers my organization had been working with prior to the drought convinced us that water was still available. They showed us how some farmers had dug shallow wells, only three to four feet deep, that enabled them to irrigate the land close to those wells. Indeed, looking down on the valley from the hills, you could see small round patches of green amid the dry and dusty landscape. The problem, they said, was getting the water farther out into the fields so they could grow enough food for themselves and their villages. The primitive rope-and-bucket method they used wouldn't do the job. What they needed were a foot-powered pump and irrigation pipes to distribute the water. Using small loans of $350, these farmers were, in fact, able to plant and eventually harvest their crops—in spite of the drought.

What was so incredible about this solution was that in addition to virtually zero defaults on those pump loans, it produced momentous ripple effects. The farmers enjoyed gainful employment and were able to offer jobs to others. They provided desperately needed food for the residents of neighboring communities. With demand high and supply low, the farmers received top value for their produce, creating capital and stimulating the economy in the valley. Further, they now owned the pumps and pipe for use in future years, should the drought continue (as it did).

The farmers gained dignity and confidence through this process. Despite the odds against them, they endured the drought and enjoyed remarkable success. Few things empower the poor, whatever country they live in, more than personal achievement. Remember, it was not our great knowledge that helped them. The farmers knew that the problem wasn't so much lack of water, but lack of a way to distribute it. Sometimes the best way to help the poor is to listen to them.

RETIREMENT IN THE DEVELOPING WORLD

Listening to a man named Raj taught me yet another lesson about the poor: not only do they want to be self-reliant, they don't want to be a burden to their families as they grow old. Each morning around five o'clock, as the sun is rising, Raj begins a half-hour trek to the wholesale market, where he loads his cart with bright red tomatoes, green cabbage, potatoes, carrots, and a variety of local squash and root crops. After washing his produce, he carefully displays it on his cart so the vegetables not only look attractive, but travel safely down the bumpy roads. With some two hundred pounds of merchandise, his return journey takes twice as long.

By seven o'clock, Raj is back in the center of town, slowly walking behind his cart and calling out the equivalent of "vegetables for sale!" He trudges up and down the streets and between the houses. The streets aren't really streets in the Western sense. They are dirt paths, often only a few inches wider than the cart itself. These paths are full of ruts and potholes, particularly during the monsoon season, when the rains in India turn the ground to a sea of mud.

Raj prefers to start his day early, with the goal of selling all his vegetables before the sun reaches its peak. He always manages the former, but late in the afternoon you will usually find him still trudging up and down the hills calling "vegetables for sale." Sometimes he's still trying to peddle his vegetables as the sun sets. He can't go home until everything is sold. Otherwise he won't have enough money to pay for his family's meal and still be able to stock his cart the next day.

After learning about his daily routine, I asked Raj the same question I have posed to so many others like him over the years: "So, Raj, how many days a week do you do this?"

While the words of his answer were slightly different, the meaning is the same as the one I get from almost all who survive at this level of extreme poverty. "I want to eat seven days."

I probed with another stock question. "What did you do with the $35 loan you borrowed for your business a year ago?" I expected to hear how he'd increased his profits by diversifying his product line, or how he cut costs by buying vegetables in bulk.

I was shocked by his response: "I bought this cart."

For seventeen years Raj had been selling vegetables from someone else's cart. That person took a large percentage of the small profit Raj made each day. Like the rickshaw operator, in seventeen years Raj had been unable to amass enough capital to buy the cart.

Now that Raj had his own cart, he made more profit, and after paying off the loan in six months, he used the extra money to expand his variety of vegetables, add some fruit, increase his profits, and shorten his workday.

Before bidding him farewell I asked Raj one final question: "What is your dream for your business?"

"I would like another loan so I can buy some lumber and build a little stall in the market," Raj replied. I smiled to myself as I realized that his response was a subtle solicitation for a subsequent loan. What entrepreneur is not always selling, or looking for more capital? Raj was no exception, despite the fact that he wanted considerably less than $100.

The reason Raj needed the wood and the shelter was at first no more evident to me than the reason behind his yearning to work seven days a week. Since he spoke no English and I no Hindi, our words were few. My ears heard what the interpreter said while my heart listened intently to the real meaning behind his words. His unspoken message went something like this:

I'm not young anymore. Here in India, at forty-seven, I'm approaching the end of my life. I'd like to retire, but that's not possible. I have no savings and no pension. There are no safety nets in my country, even for the elderly. If I don't work, I don't eat.

Selling vegetables is what I know. But I can't push this heavy cart in the blistering sun, from sunrise to sunset, up these bumpy hills much longer. If I had lumber, I could make a small shelter. I could stand in the shade and sell my vegetables in the open market.

People would come to me. No longer would I have to walk up and down the streets calling out all day "vegetables for sale." From the shade of my stall, I could sell all kinds of fragile, juicy fruit too. At the end of the day when it is time to go home, I could lock the stall and leave the remaining produce safely inside. I could make more money in less time with less strain on my aging body. And I could lease my cart to someone younger who could sell from door to door.

Most of all, I would not be a burden to my family. I sacrificed much to put each of my children through school and to help them gain self-confidence and self-reliance. They are making independent lives for themselves and their own children. They have hope for a brighter future now, and I don't want to depend on them yet. Sooner or later they will take care of me. That is how it should be. But for now they must take care of their own children and get them through school. So, you know, the wood is really to educate my grandchildren, to break this bondage of poverty for my family, and to remain self-reliant. That's all.

That's all? Speechless, I tried to appreciate the full scope of this man's dream. A few dollars doesn't just buy a little wood, it buys freedom from dependency. Along with self-reliance come dignity and self-esteem, what every soul cedes when they want, and should be able, to care for themselves but cannot. That was his heart's desire, and shockingly, to a great extent, it was mine to grant.

Poor people the world over don't want handouts. They dream of the day when they can think as big as the sky, using their own hard work and ingenuity to fulfill their dreams.

7

FAITH

When there are no safety nets,

faith takes on new meaning.

Having grown up in South Africa, the child of Christian missionary parents, I could be accurately described as a lifelong Christian. Years of Sunday school and church attendance, and even some college-level courses, have given me a solid foundation in the Bible and theology. What I have learned from the poor about faith is not so much theoretical as practical. One of the most striking differences between the faith of the poor and my own faith is the simple trust and unwavering belief of those who live in poverty. They have given me new insights into how faith can positively affect my daily life. Before I share those insights, I want to make one disclaimer.

Although I continue trying to follow the teachings of Jesus, and live as I believe he would want me to, I recognize that many readers come from other faith backgrounds—or from no faith background. Because of my upbringing and life experiences, my examples and lessons all come from Christians. This should not suggest that people of other faiths do not have similar stories to tell, miraculous events to recount, or lessons to teach. This is not a book about theology or a defense of the Christian faith. Rather, it is an account of the lessons I'm learning from the poor people I've met. It reflects my personal journey of faith, including my evolving understanding of God's special love for the poor.

WHEN GOD IS ALL YOU HAVE

Throughout North America, Great Britain, and Europe—in nations that once led the world with their vibrant Christian communities—church attendance is declining. In many developing nations, the trend is just the opposite. Not only are churches growing there, some of the largest Christian churches in the world are there. Many developing nations are sending out missionaries to other countries. And ironically, even though fewer and fewer people are going to church in the developed West, our interest in spirituality is increasing. I'm no expert on these things, but I think that one reason for this is that many of us in the West have settled for a safe Christian faith. Believing in God and going to church are nice things to do, but because of our relative affluence and individualism, we don't really *need* God. Moreover, many Christians, both Catholic and Protestant, have quietly left the institutional church because it has become too identified with political parties and issues. It has placed too much emphasis on elaborate buildings and celebrity pastors. It has suffered embarrassing scandals, and for many people has become irrelevant. Yet these "Christians in exile" still seek spiritual meaning and significance, and that's where they could learn from the faith of the poor.

Because the poor have so little, they understand what it means to trust God completely for everything. A few years ago, I was attending a conference in the Philippines along with some three hundred others from forty countries, all Christians and all involved in microenterprise development. I needed to return home a day early and was blessed at the conference to meet a Filipino couple who had driven the two hours from Manila to the retreat center and who also needed to return to the city before it was over. At about ten o'clock at night, I set out with these strangers in their clean but ever-so-used car.

About halfway to Manila the car started sputtering, jerking, and decelerating. The driver downshifted several times to keep from stalling, and we limped along in first gear at about five miles per hour. I will never forget the spontaneous response of the couple in the front seat, who without missing a beat both instantaneously started talking out loud to God. "Praise your holy name. We worship you. We give you thanks. Hallelujah. Blessed be the Lord. Thanks be to God." Back and forth they offered prayers of thanks to their heavenly Father. No cussing. No wringing of hands. No arguing about whose fault it was. No mention of the fact that we were driving through an unsafe and violent area. Not even a debate as to what course of action to take. It was a given. Total, natural trust in the divine.

For the next thirty minutes they continued praising God aloud. I sat in the back seat in quiet amazement and wonder. They did not talk to me or to each other, just to God. There were no truck stops or gas stations with twenty-four–hour service, no cell phones, and very few other vehicles. Through the pitch darkness, for half an hour we nudged slowly ahead.

Eventually whatever was causing the problem seemed to correct itself, and the car gradually started running more smoothly. After another half hour the driver gingerly shifted into second gear. A few minutes and more prayers later, he shifted into third. Once we were finally in high gear and traveling at normal speed, the couple stopped praying and apologized profusely to me for all the inconvenience they had created. I was humbled by their faith. Like many American Christians, I had it backward. Going to God is usually my last course of action when things go wrong, perhaps because I have so many other options. These people didn't. All they had was their faith.

Was the car miraculously fixed by God? There would be as many opinions about that as there are theologians. All I know is that as soon as the car started sputtering, these people started praying. What's interesting is that I don't recall them ever asking God to fix their car. They just praised and thanked God, submitting themselves to his goodness and power. God used this couple to illustrate something I had always been taught but never believed as strongly as I should have: God is sufficient, trustworthy, dependable, and wants to be the first place I turn in times of need.

SILO SPIRITUALITY

The poor have also taught me that faith is for the whole person. It is not something compartmentalized in our spiritual lives. In the United States, we are much more inclined to separate our lives into physical, emotional, and spiritual silos. We take medicines for physical complaints, go to therapy for emotional problems, and for our spiritual needs, attend church on Sundays, or at least on Christmas and Easter. The poor have a much more holistic view of faith. Things of the spirit coexist seamlessly with the physical world. The poor depend on God not only for their eternal security but also today's food and safety. They recognize that God cares about both and is an active agent in all dimensions of this life and the afterlife.

The connectedness between the spiritual and physical is by no means limited to those of the Christian faith. In many rural villages in Africa, the tribal witch doctor is still the most revered individual. With few pharmaceuticals available, when someone becomes ill, it is common to visit a witch doctor and have her or him discern how the ancestral spirits have been offended. For a fee, the witch doctor will prescribe a potion to appease the spirits and cure the ailment.

Similarly, with no lawyers available, when someone receives unfair treatment, the witch doctor might cast a spell that can result in unimaginable hardship for the accused party. In such cases, the accused must pay a defending witch doctor to cast an offsetting spell to neutralize the potency of the first. The costs can be high, but not to pay can be far more costly, given the irrefutable power and warranted reputation of some witch doctors.

I'm certainly not making a case for witchcraft; rather, I share this practice to show how comfortable the poor are with blending the spiritual and the physical. We view the spiritual world as somewhere "out there." The poor know that it is always present and active.

For them, faith is not an add-on, but a vital part of their everyday lives. When the women who receive loans gather for their weekly trust group meetings, they always include some form of spiritual expression— usually dancing, singing, and praying to God—even as they report on their respective businesses. These practices are not forced or orchestrated, but are a natural extension of who the women are as human beings, dependent on God for everything. Some may be Christians and others Muslims, but together they freely express their thanks for God's provision and protection.

In our Western culture we regularly ask God to "give us this day our daily bread," but do we really depend on him to do so? Don't we view our assets as *ours* rather than gifts from God? We assume ownership since we have earned the assets. We believe we are free to do what we think is appropriate with what is ours. The truth is, all the earth's resources belong to the one who created them. I am merely a temporary steward of what may belong to me legally. God is the true owner of all that I have claimed as mine. I am to invest and use it wisely, but it's not mine to keep.

This truth requires a paradigm shift. I am much more comfortable with the notion that what I put in the offering plate on Sunday, or the contributions I make to charity, belong to God, while the rest is mine to use as I please. What a stunted view. All my possessions belong to God. I can use some of them to sustain myself, save for the future, invest to make them grow, or give to others in need. But I do this with the understanding that the resources I am dealing with are not mine. As a steward of God's assets, I will ultimately be held accountable to him for how I manage them.

FAITH AT WORK

We may do our best to keep faith and business separate, but many of the working poor I've met do just the opposite. Eduardo Voltran is a tailor in El Salvador. He learned his trade from his father on an old pedal-operated sewing machine. Eventually Eduardo upgraded by purchasing a used electric model. He expanded his enterprise until the San Salvador earthquake of 1986 rattled his country and collapsed part of his house, crushing his sewing machine and destroying his business.

Since commercial banks don't make loans to peasants who have no capital or collateral, Eduardo was relieved to hear about a lending program from his neighbor. Based on his neighbor's good reference and his own sewing experience, Eduardo qualified for a larger loan of $1,000. With it he bought a new machine, an electric iron, and some raw material. The shop was reopened, and Eduardo was back in business. In a year the loan had been repaid. With his profits he soon purchased a better machine with more features and greater versatility. Increased productivity enabled him to hire someone to run the older machine, allowing the two of them to take on larger orders and increase sales.

When I visited Eduardo four years later in his small cinder block home, I found five machines with a worker seated behind each. Every morning Eduardo, his wife, and their three children would roll up their straw sleeping mats and move them, along with the rest of their bedding, from the cement floor to a corner. When the children left for school, Eduardo would pull out the machines, and the two hundred-square-foot single room was converted into his tailoring business. The room was used not only for production but also for sales to walk-in customers. Eduardo's shop was also serving large companies, filling bulk orders to manufacture workers' uniforms. Business was good, and Eduardo thanked God that he could also provide jobs to neighbors. Remember, his business was his home. This versatile scenario is common practice worldwide, where the tiny homes of poor families double as places of work.

What was especially impressive about Eduardo's situation was that at the end of the work day several times a week, after the sewing machines were returned to the perimeter of the room and the family had finished their evening meal, the little house was converted a third time. This time, family members brought out a stack of rough wooden benches and set them in rows. The house/business now became a church, where Eduardo held services for people in his neighborhood. Though uneducated, he served as their volunteer spiritual director, living out his conviction that the spiritual and the physical are intrinsically integrated. He knew that his house and his talents belonged to God and he gladly offered them back in simple ways.

When it comes to faith, there is little difference between Sunday and Monday, or between church and home. God is everywhere and wants to be a central part of our lives.

BALI SPIRITUAL HIGH

Half a world away in Indonesia, I met another godly man who likewise did not delineate between the physical and the spiritual, and whose life demonstrated uncompromising dependence on God. Guntur, as he was called, had been responsible for bringing a job-creation program to his rural village some twenty years earlier. Having witnessed a microfinance project on the island of Bali, where he grew up, he formed a small nongovernmental organization and served as its voluntary board chair. Guntur was also a minister who had received training from a Bible school. He felt called by God to move from his home in the booming metropolises of Bali to a remote and isolated village a thousand miles away and establish a church. With no salary available from the young church, he simply trusted God to meet his needs. That faith, however, did not keep him from also exercising his natural entrepreneurial instincts. Like Eduardo in El Salvador, he blended his physical enterprise and spiritual ministry.

Noting the perpetual construction taking place as virgin jungle was transformed into a small town, Guntur started a brick-manufacturing business. Shortly thereafter, he began making cement pavement blocks, and later clay roof tiles. He never took a stipend from the church, and though he remained poor, he was able to live off of his business's meager profits and meet his family's basic needs.

Guntur exercised his entrepreneurial skills yet again as he began planting churches in neighboring villages and training their new pastors. In each village where a church was started, he arranged for microenterprise loans to be made to church members as well as to many of the Muslim people living in the surrounding communities.

During the week I stayed with Guntur, he and his wife slept on the floor in a detached room off the rear of the house, insisting I take their room with the family's only bed. He eagerly showed me their recently completed church, which seated about six hundred people. Though extremely simple—a tin roof, concrete floor, no glass in the window openings, and crude, backless wooden benches—it was a magnificent structure in this little village. He proudly told me that the offerings of the poor members of this church had paid for virtually the entire building. From his microfinance organization, many members had received tiny business loans, business training, and the encouragement to give the first fruits of their labor back to God. Because nearly all their clients repaid their loans, over the years the organization had recycled the funds many times, putting more people in business and creating more capital for the community and church.

Curious that almost all the funds for the building had come from voluntary gifts of church members, I asked Guntur about the source of the remainder of the money. Knowing how poor he and everyone in this fledgling village was, I assumed it must have come from some mission agency abroad or at least some wealthy Christians in Bali. Guntur's response astounded me. Out of gratitude for all the jobs that had been created by loans from Guntur's organization, not only for Christians but also for Muslims, the Muslim leader of this remote village had donated all the lumber for the roof.

What a testimony of the transforming impact of God's love. Here in Indonesia, the largest Muslim nation in the world, in an almost exclusively Muslim community where any attempt to build a Christian church would typically be met with great hostility, the leading official and his entourage attended the ribbon-cutting dedication and celebration of this church. To this day, on a roof generously provided by grateful Muslims, stands a large wooden cross, the symbol of Jesus' death, resurrection, and deity. When people are poor, they tend to depend more on God. And when they do, God provides.

Due to inadequate electric service and daily blackouts throughout the region, we spent most evenings at Guntur's home talking by candlelight. Through an interpreter, he relayed fascinating tales of God's miraculous and faithful provision. Guntur had come to this jungle island to start a church. With no job, no savings, no guarantee of income, no financial backing, and no existing parish or congregation, he had no alternative but to depend solely on God. And God delivered in unexpected ways.

The church I visited was only one of five that Guntur planted and shepherded. There were not enough trained ministers to go around, and without public or private transportation, people in neighboring towns would not walk more than a few miles to attend church. Each week Guntur would get on his bicycle and ride miles down dirt footpaths to visit each of his congregations, carrying the sacraments and a message from God's written Word.

Guntur described an occasion when he was making the trek to one of his more distant churches to lead the new congregation in a special Easter service. Heavy rains the previous night had turned the jungle paths into a sticky clay mess. Every hundred yards or so he was forced to stop and clear the mud that had built up in the chainguard and under the fenders of his bike, preventing the wheels from turning. He considered turning back but had already traveled half the distance. So, knowing that these isolated Christians would be eagerly waiting for him, he pressed on.

After he had scraped off the wet clay several times, the chainguard snapped and wedged its way into the chain and wheel. The bike would not move, and he could not ride any farther. There wasn't a single person or building to be seen in any direction. Guntur examined the problem and realized that, without tools, there was nothing he could do to repair the damage. He was about to abandon his bicycle and travel the remaining miles down the muddy path on foot when two men with a large toolbox stepped out of the bush. Before he could ask them where they were from or what they were doing there, without a word, they took out their tools and began fixing his bicycle. They completed the project and packed up. Guntur bent over to see exactly what they had done to his bike. When he stood up to thank them, they were nowhere to be seen.

What do I make of Guntur's story? One option is to deny that it happened and accuse this godly servant of being either dishonest or delusional. Another option is to assume that the two men coincidentally happened to emerge from the jungle at just the right moment and just as abruptly took off into the sunset. Or is it possible that God sent two angels to care for one of his faithful children who had no other place to turn and who lived a life of total dependence on him? Throughout the developing world, regardless of the country, the poor would agree with the latter explanation.

PRAYING IN THE SPIRIT

I might still be debating the answer to that question today were it not for an experience of my own that happened more than ten years ago. I had visited the Taj Mahal the previous day, having taken that memorable rickshaw ride described in the opening scene of chapter one, when I was overcome by the injustice of the rickshaw operator's life in contrast to mine. Alone in my hotel room in a city of millions of people just as poor as my rickshaw operator, I experienced a connection with God I had never felt before. The smorgasbord of my personal spiritual journey through many denominations had not prepared me for this.

It began at four in the morning on March 30, 1999. I couldn't sleep. After three days in India my body had still not adjusted to the jet lag. My type-A personality wanted to get up and do something that mattered, but I had lost the power pack to my laptop on the flight from Chicago, so I couldn't check my email or do any other work. Rather than get up, I decided to linger in the darkness and talk to God about what I had learned from the rickshaw operator.

As I lay on my back in bed talking aloud to God, for some unknown reason I decided to do something I had never done before. I fully extended my arms with my hands to the ceiling, and in this unusual position, I started praying for individuals with whom I had been discussing my work among the poor, particularly those I couldn't seem to influence. As each person from back home came to mind, I spoke their name and pictured myself placing my outstretched hand on their head. One by one, I prayed for approximately one hundred individuals.

As I prayed for this group of affluent investors and prospective supporters, I started thinking about the unfathomable masses of humanity I had encountered in the last few days. I thought again of the rickshaw driver, and again I began to cry, just as I had when he jumped off the rickshaw to push it up a hill. "So many poor people," I said aloud to God repeatedly, raising my voice. Soon I was sobbing, shouting to, and perhaps at, God. I imagined the accumulated wealth of the people I had just named, easily in the billions of dollars. "So much money," I called to God several times.

Never in my life have I prayed so intensely. It seemed almost as if someone else were praying through my body. My arms, hands, and fingers were stretched upward. I envisioned a vast amount of money being channeled through me from the group of people for whom I had just prayed.

My arms were getting tired, but I didn't want to lower them. I reflected on the way God had worked miraculously through Moses as long as his arms were raised, and how Moses instructed others to hold up his arms during the battle so that God would continue his deliverance. Sensing that God was doing something special, I asked him to bring to my mind other people for whom I should pray.

I was reminded of the movie "Schindler's List" and how agitated Schindler became as he groped for names to expand his list of Jews who could be saved from death and the concentration camps. As I recalled new names and raised them up to God, I felt strongly drawn to some of them, cool toward several, and affectionate about others.

As I prayed, I asked God to "take it from them." Not to make these wealthy people poor, but rather to bless them, their businesses, and their stock portfolios so they might share their gifts. Eventually, the list seemed complete, and I again began praying for the poor, envisioning millions of rickshaw drivers and others like them.

Then, my wrists began shaking violently. It was as if my hands were rain clouds ready to burst open, and a deluge began to pour out over all India as the stored-up wealth was unleashed for the poor.

Gradually, as my wrists became steady again, I imagined the heavy downpour giving way to a long, gentle, and nourishing rain, the accumulated wealth raining down on these whom God loves so very much.

If this sounds strange to you, it was unlike anything I had ever experienced in my life. I sensed God was doing something bizarre but very meaningful, and I didn't want to stop him.

With my hands still in the air, I pictured God holding the earth, loving all its inhabitants. I saw the most beautiful picture I have ever imagined—the Creator tenderly holding our planet like a mother cradles her infant. So much love. So gentle. So protective. So in control.

I felt God comforting me with the truth that everything I had seen belongs to him. I found myself slowly repeating the words I sensed God saying to me: "It's all mine." All the people. All the poverty. All the wealth. I didn't have to worry. He wanted me to let go of my obsession with raising money for the poor and just be faithful. He is in control. He loves the poor more than I can begin to imagine. Never in my life have I felt such love and deep peace. While compassionately holding the whole earth, my loving Father was also embracing me. For several minutes I lay in my bed silently, basking in God's presence.

As quickly as it had begun, it was over. Ever so slowly, I lowered my weary arms. The instant my elbows hit the sheet, a bird sang outside my window. Then it was silent again. It was as if God had put his exclamation mark on our time together, signaling that the intercession was over. Then I folded my hands, physically drained but spiritually exhilarated.

SPIRITUAL SOLIDARITY WITH THE POOR

Our loving God hates poverty. He created humankind to live in a garden of plenty. He provided laws and guidelines for life so that no one would go without food and all could meet their basic needs.

Jesus showed his solidarity with the poor through his teaching, parables, and lifestyle. It is no coincidence that in his very first recorded message he referenced the poor. We're told that when Jesus went to the synagogue in Nazareth after his baptism, he selected one passage from the scroll that was handed to him. Imagine God incarnate making his human debut and selecting one message from the Hebrew Scriptures to begin his teaching ministry. The words Jesus read came from the book of Isaiah where Jesus' mission was prophesied: "The Spirit of the Lord is on me, because he has anointed me to preach good news to the poor . . . to release the oppressed." After this poignant reading, we are told by St. Luke that Jesus simply "rolled up the scroll, gave it back to the attendant and sat down," as if to say, "That's all." That is how Jesus chose to begin his ministry. His good news is for everyone, and we must read on to understand his full teaching. A central theme of Jesus' message is freeing the oppressed.

Perhaps it was the extreme degradation I witnessed in India that opened my heart to such an intense encounter with God's Spirit. What I have learned from poor Christians is that they often enjoy a more personal relationship with God than I do. It is something I long for, but when we have so much, we often miss opportunities to trust God so completely that he visits intimately with us.

The God I talked to during my prayer in India loves all his creation deeply, particularly the men and women he made in his own image, and especially those who are poor and oppressed. It grieves him greatly to see the inhumane conditions under which so many of his children toil.

If I, one of those made in God's image, cry when I get a small glimpse into the life of one rickshaw driver, what must God feel when in his omniscience he looks down on the entire planet and sees the desperate poverty of so many people over the ages—men, women, and children whom he uniquely formed and passionately adores.

I don't understand why God speaks more clearly to me when I am in the developing world, but he often does. Perhaps it is because I am away from the distractions and noise that deaden my spiritual ears and prevent me from hearing the one who said, "Be still and know that I am God." Or perhaps it is because I am more acutely aware of poverty and become sensitized to something that breaks God's heart, the plight of the poor. Or perhaps it is because he wants me to be a messenger and bring back some of the lessons he has taught the poor and wants us to learn.

Whatever the reason or combination of reasons, whenever I arrive in a developing country, like Moses before the burning bush, I take a moment of reverence to symbolically take off my sandals, knowing that the ground I stand on is holy. When I pray among the poor, I listen more intently. Perhaps it is because in those radically different surroundings, both physically and emotionally, I am more spiritually awake to God's voice and teaching.

When I am with a poor and godly couple who drive a dilapidated beater through a violent area in the Philippines, I learn what it means to depend completely on God. When I choose to live a life of dependency, even for a short time, in an isolated region of Indonesia as Guntur did, God miraculously shows up. When I am in Eduardo's multifunctional home in El Salvador, I realize how seamlessly the physical and spiritual dimensions of life are interconnected. When I let go of the self-imposed burden to eradicate poverty, I welcome God's reassuring words, "It's all mine."

8

INNOCENCE

Childhood is a luxury we must fight to protect.

In just about every urban center in the developing world you will find vendors hawking their goods—everything from food to cigarettes. Many of these peddlers abandoned the sidewalks long ago and now sell their wares in the center of the busiest intersections, mindless of traffic. Even the light changing from red to green does not abort a sale for these tenacious hawkers. Initially walking, then running, they strike deals and sell through open car windows. For them, caution and timidity mean an empty stomach.

A different type of street vendor feels more comfortable sitting cross-legged on the sidewalk, neatly displaying merchandise in front of her: a basket of tomatoes, a tray of dried fish, a colorful variety of shoelaces. These salespeople function at the bottom of the retail market chain. Their entire inventory consists of one or two items, typically the same items someone else is peddling only a few steps away. Each of these vendors knows that whatever sells today provides for tonight's meal, and hopefully leaves enough to buy a meager supply of the same limited product to sell tomorrow.

A small piece of fabric often marks the boundaries of these "stores." This cloth not only serves as a floor to sit on, but also limits the space where other would-be hawkers may want to set up their goods. We use a similar method here in the United States when we attend an outdoor concert or an Independence Day parade: we stake our claim to a section of grass by covering it with a picnic blanket or an old tablecloth. That piece of real estate belongs to me and my kin until the event is over. No one dares to set foot on a stranger's blanket!

On the streets of Manila, the small fabric square generally hosts not only a woman and her inventory, but one or two small children as well. Just as I sit in the park on my blanket enjoying my children, the Filipino mother may nurse an infant while a slightly older sibling rests quietly at her side.

THE LOSS OF POTENTIAL GENIUS

I confess that the first time I saw a mother and her young family seated together like this, I thought, *Oh, how cute*. But I quickly realized this wasn't a developing-world version of "Take Your Child to Work Day." It happens every day, all day. Kids who should be in school or playing on a swing set sit in this cramped space beside their mother as she tries to sell enough items to buy food for the day's meal. Yes, the kids are cute and, yes, there is something charming about seeing a little family together like this . . . until you begin to think about what it must be like for these children.

When I first noticed this troubling phenomenon, I was staying for a few days at a hotel in Manila. When I left in the morning, I walked past a woman and her two children sitting on a dirty blanket. After my appointments, I headed back to the hotel, and there they were—in almost the same position as when I had passed them eight hours earlier. The next morning, there they were again. And so on, for all the days I was at the hotel. Rarely did I see those children whine or fuss or tug to go play.

I initially thought to myself, *What well-behaved children!* But as I pondered their good manners, it hit me: *They've lost their childhood.* How sadly their uneventful days blend together. From birth, these children have been conditioned to endure monotony, and now they sit, almost comatose, with the innate desire to run, play, and laugh sucked out of them. How can they possibly grow into creative, problem-solving, productive adults? How many Einsteins, Shakespeares, and Mother Teresas has the world unwittingly lost, their genius and potential heroic efforts left to languish on a piece of fabric on the streets of some developing nation?

Most of the lessons I have learned from the working poor have been positive. But as I've observed the lives of their children, I've learned one of the saddest lessons of all: carefree innocence is a luxury the poor cannot afford. Hundreds of millions of children around the world learn far too early that life is filled with disappointment and despair. Almost from birth they learn that each day is a struggle to stay alive—not just for their parents, but for them as well. Born with the same intrinsic potential my children had at birth, there is little opportunity for them to blossom and develop in the absence of adequate physical, emotional, and intellectual stimulation. Many will never see the inside of a school, will never learn to read, will never learn childhood games. Is it any wonder that you seldom see children laughing in the slums of Brazil? It is the robbery of innocence that puts those blank, hopeless stares on the little faces of children who should not have to grow up so fast.

NO TIME FOR CHILDHOOD

On my first visit to India some twenty years ago, I met a group of young boys called ragpickers. Abandoned by their parents and ranging in age from seven to adolescence, these children live together on the streets in packs. Neither lazy nor corrupt, they are industrious, resourceful, and hardworking survivors of a ravaged culture. At a time in their lives when they should be signing up for afterschool soccer or enjoying special outings with family, they are already working twelve-hour days.

One boy, whom I'll call Rachid, begins each day at sunrise. He canvasses the streets and rifles through garbage set out the night before. Because these communities offer no official garbage service, millions of residents simply place their trash on the side of the road, where it remains. Rachid doesn't seek food scraps. He knows such luxuries are nonexistent in this harsh environment. Rather, he gathers whatever he can sell or recycle.

Sadly for Rachid, slum residents do not discard much. But he and his fellow ragpickers never fail to inspect the little that is discarded. They glean debris daily, even during monsoon rains. After Rachid collects his findings in a large nylon bag, he separates the plastic from the glass, metal, and paper. With the bulging sack slung over his shoulder, he resembles Santa Claus after he's slid down one too many sooty chimneys. Rachid and the other filthy boys hike to the designated recycling center where, in exchange for their morning's efforts, they receive breakfast around ten a.m. Then they head back to the streets, where they repeat the process for an evening meal. If they don't show up with enough recycled trash to earn a meal, they don't eat.

Without a positive adult influence or a nurturing family, Rachid has no one to kiss his knee and lovingly apply a Band-Aid when he falls down. He receives no education. He does not have clean drinking water or sanitation. No one provides him with safe shelter or security of any kind. Rachid has no roots and no future. He's never attended school, kicked a ball, slept in a real bed, taken a hot bath, worn a new garment, received any medicine, or known the comfort of an adult's embrace.

I sometimes wonder, do children like Rachid *ever* have even the briefest period of innocence? Was there ever a time when they experienced the carefree exhilaration and security of being a child? At what point did someone decide they could not be innocent?

No child should have to experience, no society should permit, and no loving individual should excuse the poverty and abandonment of India's ragpickers. Yet this inhumane and hellish lifestyle constitutes the daily routine of thousands of unfortunate children.

Tragically, another large group of children in India would not regard ragpicking as a life of misery, but one of freedom, independence, and hope. This group of children has been literally sold into indentured servitude. Although it is illegal in India, as well as in other poor nations, this form of slavery is widely practiced. UNICEF estimates that in Haiti alone, more than 300,000 children have been offered up by their families to a life of bondage. As the gap between rich and poor widens, destitute parents increasingly come to the tragic realization that they have something of value they can sell: their children.

To most of us, selling a child is inconceivable. How could a mom or dad knowingly hand a child over to someone in exchange for a few dollars? Because child slavery is illegal, and to better illustrate how this horrific practice happens, I have pieced together the only composite story in this book, based on several situations I've encountered.

THE SINGHS GO INTO DEBT

A couple in India, Hassan and Mariam Singh, have sacrificed dearly for years in order to ensure their oldest child receives an education. Unfortunately, the public school will not allow their son, Youssef, to take his final exam until the family pays his school fees—a mere $10 that they don't have. Though they dread the thought of dealing with Said, the neighborhood moneylender, they also feel it would be foolish not to take a loan after their years of hard work. The Singhs agree to repay the $10 plus an additional $10 at the end of the month. They recognize the usurious rate—100 percent interest per month (not annually!) but have no other option, as commercial banks refuse to lend to people like them. And Youssef's education might provide him with a better job that would benefit the entire family.

As often happens in these situations, the Singhs are unable to pay back their loan, so they continue to take out more loans. As pleased as Said is to receive their steady business, he has worked the trade long enough to know when to cut bait. He might never see his initial $10, let alone the accumulated interest, so he refuses to refinance the loan and demands full and immediate payment of $40. Said doesn't have to express an ultimatum or threaten the family—his reputation and business tactics are notorious.

The couple visits the one person who might be able to help them out of their predicament, a kiln owner who employs many laborers at his quarry and many more at his brick kiln. Mr. Dasari hires workers who have no education or skill, only a willingness to work long, hard hours in hot conditions. The indebted couple agrees to hand over their second-oldest child, a daughter named Aya, to Mr. Dasari's quarry, where for the next two months she will live and work to earn enough money for her parents to pay off the loan shark. By day Aya toils in the quarry, and at night she sleeps in the cramped barracks with the other workers.

By the sixth week, her malnourished and dehydrated body no longer allows her to produce even one brick per day. Mr. Dasari contacts the Singhs, telling them he has to buy medicine for their daughter. They agree that he can keep her for two additional months in exchange for the medication she clearly needs. To show his concern for her well-being, and to seal the new contract, he allows Aya two days off from working in the quarry, while he continues to feed her as if she had put in the full amount of work.

After a couple of days of shade and rest, Aya returns to the quarry, with two and a half months of debt remaining. When her younger brother dies and her parents need money for the funeral, her term is extended by another year. Several mishaps and even more years later, both Aya and her parents wonder if she will ever come home.

Though it takes the Singhs several years to concede that they might never see their daughter again, the kiln owner has long since reached this conclusion. The realization gives him the confidence to hold firm in his strict demands when the Singhs' next family emergency strikes. Since the family is so poor, emergencies are a way of life. Despite fervent efforts to scrape up enough money to buy back their daughter, something always goes wrong. Both the loan sharks and disreputable business owners know there is no margin for error, so they rely on the family's continuing misery to stay in business.

Their oldest child remains the couple's only hope of redeeming their beloved daughter. Immediately after finishing tenth grade, Youssef apprentices in a tool-and-die business owned by Ibrahim. In lieu of a salary, Ibrahim provides food and lodging, and promises eventual partnership in the business. Such advancement should allow Youssef to redeem his sister from bondage and enable him to care for his parents during their later years. But for the period of apprenticeship, Youssef will not be able to contribute to the family income.

Ibraham's tool-and-die shop flourishes. But the little shop does not have enough electricity to run all the machines at once. Months prior, Ibrahim applied to the city for additional electrical service. Each week the city employees told him to come back the following week. The owner understood the ultimatum: if he would simply pay the expected *baksheesh* (bribe), the officials would reward him with the additional service tomorrow. If he did not, tomorrow might never come.

An astute businessman, Ibrahim had computed how much money he is losing each day that he doesn't have enough power to run all his machines. Finally, he sends Youssef to the village office with money for the service and some extra for *baksheesh*.

But now the clerk there reneges on his original offer, demanding that Ibrahim pay even more. When Youssef is unable to pay, the clerk sells information to an insider at the police station and files a report of attempted bribery and obstruction of justice. Within hours, authorities arrest and set a hefty bail for both Ibrahim and Youssef. A portion of the bond payment, split several ways, will line the already well lined pockets of the experienced clerk.

The streetwise business owner Ibrahim chalks up this additional money to the cost of doing business. He posts his bond by arranging a loan, borrowing money against one of the inoperable machines that had led to his predicament in the first place. His apprentice, Youssef, faces a more daunting problem. He cannot pay his bond.

When Youssef lands in jail, his father and pregnant mother return to the brick kiln once more to try to elicit help from Mr. Dasari. The Singhs arrive at the office for their meeting, and the brick kiln owner welcomes them with complimentary tea in plastic cups, along with an equally plastic smile. With many years of finely honed experience, he listens to their story, asking open-ended questions that extract more details than they intended to disclose about their grave misfortune.

Within minutes Mr. Dasari understands the nature of the emergency and knows the amount of Youssef's bail. Later in the conversation, he gathers additional information that could help him in future negotiations. Mr. Dasari also discovers the due date of the Singhs' baby, the precise day when Youssef will complete his apprenticeship. He learns that the Singhs are a faithful Hindu family. He finds out that they long to have several more children. Yes, this kiln owner knows a lot. And he knows that knowledge is power, and power is money. The couple has neither.

Mr. Dasari reminds the Singhs, "You will do best to accept your karma. You risk harm to yourselves and your children if you complain or fight back. But if you can persuade your children to accept whatever comes in this life, then they can have hope that in the next life they will no longer be members of this low caste."

As the Singhs stand to leave, Mrs. Singh says, "Thank you, again, for loaning us the money for our son's bail. No one else could have helped us so generously and so promptly."

Mr. Singh adds, "We hope Youssef will soon be freed, and with his earnings, so will Aya."

Hassan and Mariam leave Mr. Dasari's office grateful for the encouraging lesson their god wanted the kiln owner to speak into their lives. Upon leaving, however, they have accrued a monumental item in the debit column of their account. They must return on the fifth birthday of their unborn child to leave him or her to work for two years in the quarry. If anything should happen to prevent the child from engaging in manual labor, whether an accident or an injury intentionally inflicted by either of the child's parents, then the debt will be transferred double-fold to the child born of their next pregnancy.

Several years go by. Aya is too worn down and diseased to be of further value to Mr. Dasari. By now, he has manipulated the couple in many sinister ways to keep them in debt. He even strikes a deal to receive a percentage of Youssef's earnings, limiting the boy's ability to improve his family's standard of living. It's hard to imagine that in the twenty-first century we tolerate such barbaric behavior. But millions of families in the developing world today face horrific variations of this diabolical scenario. Like vultures, men like Mr. Dasari prey upon the helpless parents of able-bodied children to obtain what is essentially free labor. In what seemed a noble, though desperate, effort to help one child get an education, an entire family paid dearly for their Faustian bargain.

BEFORE YOU THROW STONES

When we hear stories like this, it's easy to cast judgment on all the guilty parties: the loan sharks, exploitative businessmen, the clerk, even the parents. How could anyone treat a child this way? The universal question is "Why?" Why did this happen? Why did no one help? Our own attitudes and self-absorption often make us deaf, dumb, and blind to the suffering of others both near and far away. We do not see the world with the eyes and heart of God. I am haunted by the way my own indifference sometimes creeps into my behavior.

Once, with time to kill, I was walking through an open market in Guatemala City, searching for gifts to take home. I came upon a little girl. Powerless in the world's eyes, she still managed to cast a spell on me that lingers many years later. With big brown eyes and bushy pigtails like carrot tops on either side of her head, she looked to be about five years old, but most likely was ten. In those first years of her life, she had probably eaten only half of what healthy children eat.

With her broken English, which was far better than my nonexistent Spanish, she began to strike up a conversation.

"Hello, nice man."

The little girl, who carried her merchandise in a broad, flat straw basket on top of her head, carefully lowered it to show me the contents: woven vests, quilted potholders, an embroidered purse, knitted socks, and colorful cloth belts. Her mother had handmade each item. The girl had apparently learned from other street vendors that this unique selling feature makes products irresistible to tourists who are looking for something authentic to take home.

To this day, I can't imagine who buys all those woven vests, as there seemed to be more for sale in that one small market than there were people in Guatemala. Who would wear the traditional garment other than the Maya peasants themselves? The locals did not, and, certainly, foreigners would not.

Still, the traditional skills, both of making and of selling, are proudly passed from one generation to the next. Every Maya girl learns the trade, and consequently every older woman weaves vests, hoping to be the one lucky saleswoman whose product appeals to the token tourist that day.

Frankly, I wasn't interested. And judging from the sheer number of unsold vests in the market, others tourists felt the same way. A seasoned vendor, the little girl noticed my lack of interest in her vests but also saw me looking at her quilted potholders. In a few seconds, she placed in full view all five potholders, each one different, each in the shape and color of a distinct fruit.

"Nice man. Which one you like?"

I committed the rookie mistake of touching one.

"Three dollars," she said, picking it up and placing it in my hand.

When I didn't show much interest in that particular potholder and returned my focus to the pear-shaped one in her basket, she instantly reduced the price to $2. She noticed that I gave two nanoseconds' more attention to the one that looked like a slice of watermelon, and before I knew it, I held both the pear and the watermelon.

"Take two," she encouraged.

I didn't want either potholder, and, with a smile, shook my head and returned them both to her basket.

"Three for five dollars," she countered, shoving them back into my hands.

This time I withdrew my hands and uttered my first words to her, "No, thank you."

"Nice man. Take four for five dollars."

"No, thank you," I repeated and started to turn away.

"Special price for you, nice man. Take all five for five dollars."

"No thanks. I'm really not interested," I said over my shoulder as I walked off.

Without a moment's hesitation, she hoisted the basket back on her head and followed me saying, "Nice man."

I didn't answer, and kept walking. She walked closely by my side, demanding my attention. "Nice man. Please. Nice man. All five for five dollars." A few steps later, "Okay, for you, all five for four dollars. Nice man. Please."

I picked up my pace—I just wanted to move on to other vendors and try to find something else, but she wouldn't give up.

"Three dollars. Take all five for three dollars."

I walked faster. Although the distance between us grew, I could still hear her voice, "Two dollars. Five for two dollars. Please. Nice man. Two dollars."

By that time, I'd exited the market, almost running back to the hotel, and yet I could still hear her faint voice in the distance, "One dollar. Nice man. One dollar. Please. One dollar."

As I turned the corner, I spied a public bench, where I decided to sit down for few minutes and shake off the unpleasant encounter. I had enough time only to take a few deep breaths when who should come around the corner but the little girl? I sat there in disbelief, frustration, and resentment, uncertain as to how this would end.

Slowly she walked to within a foot of me. Seated, I was still taller than she. With chin raised and head tilted slightly, she looked me straight in the eyes, and this time almost in a whisper said, "Please. All five for fifty cents."

At that point I probably could have owned everything in her basket for fifty cents. Instead, evading her gaze I ended our negotiation: "No!"

Not another word was spoken. Chin lowered, she turned and walked away, with a little less self-esteem, and a lot less hope

The moment the girl rounded the corner, in my mind I heard a cock crow, loudly and mockingly, deeply piercing my sense of justice. I knew how the apostle Peter must have felt after denying Jesus. In another passage of Scripture, Jesus told his followers that whatever they did not do for the least of these, they did not do for him (Matthew 25:45). To this day, I shudder at my denial of Jesus, personified by a hungry little girl in Guatemala.

She was not stupid. She knew the raw material in each potholder cost more than ten cents. But in her case, knowledge was not power. Rather, she realized how impotent she was against the likes of me, and she was willing to sell what little she had for the price of one meal.

I had the power to buy her goods and enable her to eat with dignity. She hadn't asked for a handout. Nor was she begging. Nor was she lazy. This little girl, who should have been in school, peddled inexpensive souvenirs on the streets instead. This child, who desperately needed my supporting hand, received instead my harsh tongue. My two-letter word ended our dialogue and sent her on her way as hungry as she had been when we first met.

"Jesus, nice man, who loved the little children, who beckoned them to sit in your lap, who asked that they be brought to you for care and healing, who instructed me to do likewise—have mercy on me and forgive me, please. How it must grieve you to look down from heaven and see children suffering—to see their hunger, vulnerability, neglect, abuse, hopelessness. How your heart must break to watch their innocence and joy be taken from them. I apologize for my lack of compassion for the children of the world. Help me see them as you do: truly as the least among us. Help me respond in love as you would!"

LET THE LITTLE CHILDREN SMILE

A social worker in Jamaica told me about a priest who distributes food to the homeless in Kingston's slums. One day a bakery gave him several bags of old bread. It was too stale to sell, but too nourishing to discard. As the priest walked the streets handing out bread to those who looked to be most impoverished, he received the typical response, "Thank you, Father."

He happened upon a little boy, all alone and obviously malnourished. When he handed bread to the boy, to his surprise the shoeless, shirtless child responded not with thanks but with tears.

"What's the matter, son? Why are you crying?"

The little boy lowered his head and in one softly spoken sentence divulged the depth of their family's want. Between his sniffles the boy replied, "Today is my sister's turn to eat."

Rather than inflicting its scars uniformly upon all people, scarcity is most ruthless to the young. An infant suffers lost potential on a sidewalk in the Philippines. Homeless ragpickers struggle to survive in India. A child remains ensnared in a life of slavery. A little girl in Guatemala pesters tourists to earn a few cents. A young boy in Jamaica eats on alternating days, taking turns with his sister.

The children of the working poor have taught me a lesson I will never forget—sometimes innocence is just too expensive. Learning this truth only increases my resolve that we can, and must, eradicate extreme poverty. We have the resources to make sure that everyone has enough to eat, a place to call home, and the dignity of being able to support themselves.

We have what it takes to help a young child smile.

9

INGENUITY

The poorest entrepreneurs

redefine creativity and innovation.

As I write this book, the United States, and much of the rest of the developed world, is trying to claw its way out of a debilitating recession. Unemployment in America hovers around 10 percent and seems content to stay there. Retailers report flat sales. Companies big and small are looking for ways to cut costs. Perhaps a field trip to some of the poorest regions in the world would spark a new sense of ingenuity and increase profits here in the West. Business owners could learn valuable lessons from the working poor, guaranteed to increase revenue and profits.

Out of necessity, the world's poorest people are possibly some of the most ingenious. Many of them literally make something out of nothing and find a way to sell it. In the developing world, the unholy trinity of government, military, and remnant oligarchs devours most direct intergovernmental aid, all but erasing opportunity and the middle class. Poor entrepreneurs eke out a living on the margins, usually in businesses of fewer than ten people. A lack of possessions spurs people to unimaginable creativity as they reclaim space and recycle resources that I am quick to disregard and destroy. If gratitude is the winsome and unexpected response of many who are working their way out of chronic poverty, resourcefulness is the catalyst that propels them forward.

CASH FROM ASH

What's amazing about this resourcefulness is that it often springs up out of situations that would otherwise be considered disasters. For example, when Mount Pinatubo erupted in 1991, thousands of family businesses in the Philippines were ruined, not by hot gushing lava, but by lahars, thick mudflows formed by volcanic ash and rain. In the weeks that followed the eruption, volcanic ash fell from the sky like snow, settling several feet deep for miles around the mountain. Then the rains came and the lahars flowed down the side of the mountain through the villages where the poor lived. They buried thousands of houses and businesses.

Obviously, these poor people needed to dig out, but they took it a remarkable step further. In the aftermath of this cataclysm, an innovative business emerged that not only cleaned up the mess, but created a market for a new product that in turn helped rebuild the local economic infrastructure. Resourceful entrepreneurs began manufacturing bricks from the ash by creating a mud-like mixture, compacting it in molds, and then setting out the blocks to bake in the sun. These mud bricks were in high demand during the reconstruction of demolished neighborhoods. Manufacturing businesses were reestablished, retailers rebuilt stores, welders made gates, and bakers constructed ovens, all using bricks made of ash and mud. The ingenuity of a few people paved the way to rebuild the area's economy one brick at a time.

Or consider the ingenuity that followed the long, costly civil war in Nicaragua during the 1980s. As is the case with natural disasters, the innocent always end up poorer during wartime. Yet in the ways that natural catastrophes become the impetus for invention, so do political unrest and change. In the early '90s, after the Sandinistas had been defeated, many burned-out and destroyed Russian military vehicles were left behind on the sides of Nicaraguan roads. One entrepreneur saw an opportunity to transform the cast aluminum engine parts into practical pots and pans.

He stripped the abandoned vehicles and, with a low-tech furnace fueled by oil drained from the vehicle's engines, melted the parts. He then poured the molten aluminum into pot molds that he created from moist sand. Pieces of wire, pressed into the pot as the metal cooled, served as handles. I have one of these pots with a matching (or almost matching) lid in my office today. I imagine that it was once an engine part from a Russian Jeep and I keep it as a daily reminder of the ingenuity and frugality of the world's poor.

Every time I start my car in the winter, I'm reminded of yet another example of ingenuity among the poor. Extreme winters in Chicago take a toll on our car batteries, and when those batteries finally give out, we discard them and buy new ones. But in El Salvador, the cost of a new car battery equals 120 hours of work for a taxi driver. Rather than buy a new battery for $50, the driver is happy to pay $20 for a used one that has been rebuilt.

That's the nature of Juan's business. He knows that when the battery in a car dies and he must replace it, the problem is not that all the cells are no longer functioning, but that only a couple of the six or eight cells don't work. By visiting garages and auto dealers and scavenging through garbage, Juan finds discarded batteries. He breaks them down and determines the condition of each cell. Using working cells from several different units, he reassembles one good battery. He even stands behind his product with a written warranty.

I watched as Juan and his workers carried around and stepped over mounds of old car batteries. They had already taken the batteries apart and exposed the extremely hazardous acid. Despite this danger, the laborers wore short pants and open sandals. They had no gloves and no eye protection. Children and dogs dropped by to say hello. All this activity took place in a little open shed attached to the side of Juan's house, which is almost as small as the shed. Safety has a different priority in the developing world. I cringe at the conditions but marvel at the resourcefulness.

A COMPANY MADE OF CARDBOARD

One of the more resourceful microenterprises I have inspected was a custom box–manufacturing business in the Philippines. Benjie runs his factory out of the back of his house in a makeshift room about the size of a three-car garage. He began with six laborers. When I met him, he was already employing twelve full-time workers. By assigning them eight-hour workdays, he is able to run two shifts, generating twice as much profit from many of his fixed costs.

The simple hand-operated machines and labor-intensive production process run freely with minimal supervision. This enables Benjie to spend most of his time out marketing to his customers and filling new orders. He calls on the owners of little boutique shops in downtown Manila where specialty items are sold, many of them handmade. Benjie discovered that many of these store owners needed boxes with uncommon dimensions, and usually only a few of each size. Benjie records the measurements and the quantity of each container needed, then returns a few days later with the newly manufactured boxes. While in town, he also visits the large department stores and relieves them of their unwanted shipping cartons. He breaks down the large boxes and hauls the cardboard back to his home. At first he strapped it to a bicycle. In recent years he has been driving a very old truck that he fixed up.

Once back in the shop, Benjie adds the flattened cartons to the mounds of cardboard collected on previous days. He gives the slip of paper with the day's orders to his most seasoned employee. Somewhere in my memorabilia, I have a little tattered piece of paper that served as the order form the week I visited Benjie. Scrawled across the paper are about twenty-five rows of numbers, each with four columns. The first column is the quantity, and the other columns are the dimensions: width, length, and height, listed in centimeters.

An old carton is broken open and the cardboard placed flat, measured, marked, and cut. Benjie's employees use a hand-operated paper cutter, only slightly larger than the ones most of us are accustomed to seeing in our schools and offices. Any remaining strips and pieces of cardboard too small to reuse are placed in a pile that Benjie sells to someone else who shreds them further, then wets and presses them to produce decorative wrapping paper. The next step in Benjie's process is to score the cardboard where a worker will later fold it. Once this process is completed, someone else glues together the two outside edges, using adhesive that Benjie manufactures himself. First, though, Benjie makes sure the old box is reversed, with brand names and other printing facing inward. That way the new custom-sized box is clean and free from any distracting printing or lettering.

If you listen to the news, you would think that Americans invented recycling, but I visited Benjie's cottage industry back in the early '90s before recycling was in vogue in my Midwestern hometown. Years ahead of his time, Benjie leveraged his resources at every level, beginning with discarded cardboard. He did not use fuel-burning or even electric machines in the manufacturing process. He produced his own glue and utilized space and equipment across two shifts by employing a dozen people. And he used his old, refurbished truck to deliver products, gather supplies, and bring back orders, all in one trip. Benjie successfully identified and met a legitimate need in the market.

As I have said, business leaders in the developed world who are struggling to make ends meet could learn much from resourceful entrepreneurs like Benjie.

TASTES LIKE CHICKEN

Perhaps the zenith of ingenuity would be the ability to turn chicken droppings into profit. Setiawan was an early settler on the island of Sumatra, arriving in 1981 as part of the government's transmigration strategy to offset congestion and poverty in the urban centers of Indonesia. Setiawan migrated from Java, almost 2,000 miles to the east, and on his free five-acre plot planted coconut trees and raised cows and goats. This lifestyle of subsistence farming barely kept food on the table for his five children. When a microenterprise program came to his community, Setiawan saw the chance to carry out his vision and was one of the first to sign up. With a $500 loan, he bought hand tools and hired thirty-five people to help him dig seventeen shallow fishponds on his property. Shovels and hoes were all they used to divert water from a mountain stream before stocking his ponds with fish. Today Setiawan harvests one hundred pounds of carp a day.

He took out a second loan of $1,000 and built chicken coops on stilts above the ponds, with the floors of the coops just inches above the surface of the water. The floors were made of slats with spaces between them wide enough to allow the droppings from the chickens to fall through and feed the fish. What he once spent on fish food he now uses to buy chicken feed, and the chickens provide for the fish. The digested food that the chickens consume still contains enough nutrients for the carp to grow, providing a source of meat for consumers. Currently Setiawan is harvesting more than 1,200 chicken eggs a day and thousands of pounds of protein-rich fish.

What an impact this chicken enterprise made! It allowed three of his children to attend college, supplied nutritious food for his little village, created income opportunities for those selling his eggs, provided full-time employment for three farm workers, and trained others in the community how to replicate his farm, all the while feeding nineteen tons of carp. Not a bad return on a $1,000 investment.

When I first heard that Setiawan was training others how to raise chickens, I asked him if this was a wise move or if it might create competition and hurt his business. Obviously I forgot one of the lessons I have learned from the working poor: gratitude translates into generosity. This Muslim businessman, like James the Ghanaian goat farmer who gave one of his animals for his church's Christmas celebration, was eager to help others who were poor like him. Gratitude and generosity are not unique attributes of any single religion. I'm convinced that the poor understand these twin attributes better than anyone.

As he answered my question, Setiawan expressed his desire for another loan, this time for $1,500. With these funds he was planning to buy a corn-milling machine. Like any good entrepreneur, he was acutely aware of the external threats to the success of his business. In his case, it was ready access to chicken feed. Under current circumstances, the fish were adequately nourished by the droppings of the chickens. But should chicken feed become scarce, not only would the chickens be in jeopardy, so would the fish. His business eye could see that the dominoes were lined up too closely, and if one fell, it could trigger instant ruin.

Like so many of the working poor I have met, Setiawan was keenly aware of his market, constantly positioning himself to diversify his business and increase revenue. As he trained others how to raise chickens, this astute businessman was at the same time creating a need for chicken feed, which he knew to be in short supply.

With numerous farms in this former jungle, there was no shortage of corn. Instead, what Setiawan discovered was a weak link in the supply chain, resulting in a huge markup on corn that was prepared as chicken feed. He recognized an opportunity to mitigate that risk and the additional costs while passing on the expense of the needed grinder to others who were entering the market. Within only one season, he would be able to pay for the purchase of the corn-milling machine, gain uninterrupted access to feed for his own chickens that would then feed his fish, and create an additional, ongoing income stream through the sale of ground corn to neighboring chicken farmers.

We often dismiss the poor as uneducated and unable to create their own opportunities. I have met so many people like Setiawan who need only a chance. Their resourcefulness takes care of the rest.

NO SPACE LEFT UNUSED

One of the more interesting examples of how the poor figure out creative solutions to serious challenges that threaten their existence is their ability to find habitable space where it seemingly doesn't exist. It's that something-out-of-nothing theme again. In high-density cities like New York we are able to house millions of people in a small area simply by going up. Skyscrapers and high-rises as we know them do not exist in many cities in the developing world, and where they do, the poor cannot afford the rent. Consequently, the ultra-poor have to make do with leftover space, any sliver of land that no one else wants or can find a way to use.

The amusing song lyric "The railroad comes through the middle of the house" came to mind as I watched a huge locomotive race down the "sidewalk" of a residential community at thirty miles an hour, clearing homes by only inches. For miles on the outskirts of Manila, tin and wood shacks had been erected, three families high, immediately next to the railway tracks on both sides. The tenants were squatters, as land this close to the tracks was not available for sale or lease.

From the perspective of the homeless, however, the narrow strip of open space along either side of the tracks was available, livable, and usable land. And use it they did. The tracks now serve as the walkway separating the two rows of dwellings. They are also a playground for children, the meeting place for neighbors and lovers, open space to hang drying laundry, a stomping ground for street vendors, and space for everything else one typically does in the yard or on the street where one lives. The three-foot space between the two iron rails also serves as the workshop for furniture makers, welders, tailors, and sundry enterprises and manufacturers.

What about safety? Every forty-five minutes or so, a whistle blasts in the distance. Children and dogs rush indoors. Women take in laundry and recoil clotheslines. Merchants collapse stalls and retrieve merchandise. Manufacturers remove tools and partially completed products. Residents clear the track just in time for the speeding locomotive to barrel through the neighborhood, swaying from side to side on the uneven lines. Houses on the ground floor enjoy a generous twelve-inch clearance. Those on the third floor have no trouble either. Since they are higher than the roof of the train, some people have cantilevered their living quarters out beyond the dwelling space below them so the train actually passes under the foremost portion of their homes. Families living on the second floor are in the most precarious position. As I watched the engine and its half-dozen coaches rock back and forth, the tops of the cars came within six inches of scraping the sides of the buildings. Over the years those constructing the dwellings have no doubt experimented with just how far toward the tracks they dare extend their homes. If that six-inch gap were not periodically encroached upon by a moving train, there is no question in my mind that the houses would be placed even closer to the tracks.

Residents have also experimented with how far away the train is when the whistle blows and how fast the locomotive is traveling. I dared not ask when last a child had not cleared the tracks in time. As I noted earlier concerning the workers rebuilding car batteries, in the developing world, safety takes a lower priority than creating a source of income or finding a place to sleep and live.

Within minutes of the train passing, life returns to normal—if normal includes making a living by building a dresser between the two steel tracks on an active railroad line. In the developing world, "normal" includes pretty much any activity, in any location, that generates any income. The greater the necessity, the more ingenious the invention, including the way space is used.

For the poorest of the working poor, zoning is a nonissue. Whatever the business, the majority of those who manufacture or sell products or services conduct their enterprises from their densely packed homes. Even on the main streets, a house can be next door to a restaurant, which is crammed next to an outdoor auto mechanic, which is next to a hairdresser, and then a furniture maker, a day care center, a tavern, a brick yard, a tailor, and so forth. Most of these buildings double as homes to the families who own and operate them.

APPLYING WHAT I LEARNED

As I mentioned earlier, many businesses in the developed world could benefit from adopting the kind of ingenuity I have seen in the working poor around the world. One quick example illustrates how organizations have had to learn how to be more resourceful as conditions in the world change.

When the Iron Curtain fell in 1989, the economies in the former Soviet bloc collapsed, state factories closed, and many professional salaries fell to $50 a month or lower. For millions of people, despite ample education and extensive work experience, self-employment became the only option to stave off poverty. Suddenly, there was a need and opportunity to export entrepreneurship to people who previously could not access capital and had never been exposed to free enterprise. It was a great opportunity for a microfinance organization to step in and help, but the usual business model, created for communities in the developing world, wouldn't be effective in this context. Those of us working in microfinance had to learn from our poorer clients how to adapt and respond to this new reality.

During my time with Opportunity International in the 1990s, we realized that, to start with, microfinance loans needed to be much larger in the Soviet bloc economies, averaging $2,000 rather than $125. Second, requiring borrowers to join small trust groups for encouragement and accountability would not work in an environment where communism had virtually destroyed trust. Consequently, loans needed to be made to individuals rather than to a group whose members cross-guaranteed each other's loans. Third, though the borrowers were usually well educated, after years of dependency on the state and no understanding of the free market, a unique type of business training was needed. Consider pricing as an example. When a ticket to an evening at a renowned opera house in Moscow costs the same as a loaf of bread, how do you price whatever widget you're manufacturing?

The first loan we made outside of Africa, Asia, or Latin America went to a Bulgarian entrepreneur with an advanced degree. In 1993 Bulgaria was bankrupt, with two-thirds of all households living below the poverty line. There were few sources of capital or credit. The wealth of the country resided in its people, many with professional training and experience. Dr. Andrei Yovkov had practiced dentistry for eighteen years at a state-owned clinic where he earned less than $100 per month. Supplies were inadequate and service poor, typical of communist countries. When private practice became legal, Yovkov tried to set up a practice in his house, buying supplies as his meager salary allowed. Still, after two years, he had not saved enough money to purchase a basic dental chair.

When he applied for a $2,400 microfinance loan to buy a used Russian dentist chair, his business plan indicated he would charge $2 for a general visit. Knowing that the government-owned clinics were practically free, we questioned why anyone would choose to pay even this small fee for his service. Based on conventional business knowledge, we were skeptical of his ability to pay back the loan. But Yovkov explained that in post-communist Bulgaria, "free" was relative. In this case it meant you stood in line for several hours to see the dentist, got no Novocain no matter how much drilling and filling was involved, and had to provide payment of at least one bottle of vodka (under the table) for the privilege of getting dental work done.

We gave him the loan. One year later, Yovkov had built a proper, albeit modest, clinic. His income had tripled, and he had paid his loan off early. Had we remained entrenched in our normal way of doing things, he might never have gotten the loan. Listening and learning enabled the organization to expand its business and thus help an entire new class of working poor to become self-sustaining.

On a personal level, I might have learned too well from the poor about ingenuity. Only a couple of years after visiting the squatters along the train tracks in the Philippines and seeing Setiawan's fish and chicken farm in Indonesia, I engaged in a massive renovation project in my own home. Our old house sat on a foundation perched over a dark, damp cellar containing several supporting pillars that held up our house—basically useless space. After seeing how wisely the poor use "unusable" space, I decided to reclaim the cellar and turn it into a family room with natural lighting, adequate head clearance, appropriate humidity, and no obstructing pillars in the middle of the room.

As I tried to figure out how I was going to accomplish this dream, I thought of Setiawan. For the next two years, with the help of two high school boys, some shovels, and a wheelbarrow, I began to dig out the basement to expand its dimensions. My small dig became sixteen truckloads of dirt, excavated entirely by hand. Springtime thaws threatened to flood the workspace. Neighbors and friends began to doubt my sanity. I kept at it.

Where was all this internal energy coming from? Why was I so determined to improve our property without adding to the dimension of our house? Why this compulsion to do more with less? This notion of living in our house while building it? This confidence that the seemingly insurmountable is attainable? I was learning from the poor.

I have much more to learn about recycling and appropriately inhabiting my corner of this global village. It's obvious, too, that I already know a lot more than I am implementing. I still replace appliances and other damaged items rather than making the effort to fix them. I walk past lights that should be turned off and thermostats that should be turned down. I fail to consolidate, carpool, and conserve. When they were in college, my daughters constantly pointed out items I should have been recycling rather than discarding. Thankfully that has become more instinctive today.

To combat my lax tendencies, I regularly use a simple exercise: expressing thanks for possessions that are outdated or ready for an upgrade. For instance, at the time I am writing this, our two cars are ten and thirteen years old and have a combined 260,000 miles on them. Hitting the ten-year mark or watching the odometer advance to the sixth digit brings a sense of fulfillment. Every month or mile after that is like driving on borrowed time. As much as I enjoy the change and novelty of acquiring a different car, that pleasure is combined with a sense of failure. As I drive to work, I frequently express a quick thanks to God that my car is still running well enough and cheaply enough, without looking too disgraceful, that I don't have to replace it. This is one small way I try to identify with the poor and resist the constant temptation to possess and consume more.

If you hang out with the poor, you find your own attitudes changing. We often come up with multiple reasons why something won't work, but the poor always seem to find that one solution we ignored or thought impossible. They have to. Often, it's a question of survival. Find a way to get water to an arid field, or die of hunger. Accept the fact that you are uneducated and unemployed, use your ingenuity to figure out how to make something that someone else needs, and then sell it.

Unlike the poor, I don't need ingenuity to survive, but adopting their resourceful attitude enriches my life. They recycle because it creates income and jobs for other poor people. My recycling removes the clutter from my life and gives me the satisfaction of knowing I am not needlessly contributing to landfills. They embrace change and adaptability in order to stay alive. If I adopt that spirit, I live more freely, staying out of the rut that so many of my peers complain about.

When Monet looked at a simple haystack, he saw glorious colors and mesmerizing shadows. The poor look around their bleak environment and see opportunity. Much-needed lanterns made from old jars scavenged from garbage dumps. Floor mats from discarded scraps of cloth. Cooking pots from Jeeps. A furniture factory between railroad tracks.

This is the spirit that will help eradicate poverty.

10

AWARENESS

Thanks to technology,

the whole world is watching.

In 1968, demonstrations outside the Democratic National Convention in Chicago turned ugly when police began arresting people, ostensibly for violating the eleven p.m. curfew. Perhaps unfamiliar with the media's relatively new portable television cameras, the police liberally applied their nightsticks to the head of every person they arrested. Meanwhile, the demonstrators, perhaps a little more savvy about the press, began chanting, "The whole world is watching!"

Well, not exactly. In 1968, when it came to media coverage, the "whole world" was limited primarily to North America, Western Europe, Australia, possibly Japan, and parts of South Africa. There was no CNN and there were no satellites to take American television networks far beyond U.S. borders. Reporters working the floor of the convention wore strange-looking headsets with little antennas poking up in the air. "Live" coverage usually meant that the show was broadcast live to affiliate stations in the United States. But if you were a poor family in Ethiopia or the country then called Rhodesia, you had no idea what was going on in Chicago during the Democratic National Convention.

Today, all that has changed. With the proliferation of cell phones, the Internet, satellite communication, wireless networking, and other technological advancements, the whole world is connected. The lesson

I am learning from the poor is this: our global village is connected. The whole world really *is* watching. Our news. Our soap operas. Our advertisements. Our lives.

As a kid living in South Africa in the late 1960s, I might have heard about those riots at the Democratic National Convention a week or two after they happened. But to a teenager living in Soweto today, CNN anchor Wolf Blitzer is a household name. You can live in a squatter village in India and watch Brian Williams on the NBC evening news.

The poor have taught me that in the twenty-first century, nothing we do in the West escapes their notice. Oprah, Conan, "Avatar," the Kentucky Derby, Benny Hinn, SpongeBob, Wall Street . . . It's all out there for the whole world to see: our actions, our attitudes, and perhaps most importantly, our lifestyles.

In his book *The Fortune at the Bottom of the Pyramid,* globally recognized business consultant C. K. Prahalad describes in detail the economic activity of the world's poorest four billion people. His research confirms that these people are increasingly aware of the world's richest sectors. One community he studied was Dharavi, a shantytown outside Mumbai, India. He describes how the priorities of the poor alter the way they spend their limited resources:

> They might not spend disposable income on sanitation, clean running water, and better homes, but will spend it on items traditionally considered luxuries. Without legal title to land, these residents are unlikely to invest in improving their living quarters, much less the public facilities surrounding their homes. For example, in Dharavi, 85 percent of the households own a television set.

Strange as it may seem, when electricity is brought to a squatter village in India, one of the first appliances families purchase (sometimes even before a stove or hot plate) is a television. They may not be able to afford shoes for their children, but they will figure out a way to buy a TV or at least go in with neighbors on the purchase of one. It helps break the monotony and drudgery of their daily existence, one that is devoid of movie theaters, libraries, concert halls, dining out, ballgames, or any of the other diversions we in the West take for granted. Sometimes it's even a source of income as enterprising individuals take out loans to purchase a TV, then make the payments from the fees they charge their neighbors to watch it!

As more people in the developing world have access to television, they become aware of our Western culture and values through hours of programming produced in Hollywood. I can't recount how many shacks or hovels I have visited where there was an uninterrupted flow of reruns from shows like "Charlie's Angels," "Baywatch," or our standard soap operas, some dubbed in the local language and others simply droning on in English. No doubt, as you read this, residents of Outer Mongolia are digesting reruns of "Desperate Housewives."

People who have never held the equivalent of a $10 bill watch people in the West repeatedly gorge themselves on fast food. They observe as we nonchalantly sip an exotic martini that costs many times their day's wage. They notice how a person idly passes time in extravagant shopping sprees at glitzy malls. The poor in the developing world are painfully aware of our affluent lifestyles and the stark contrast to their drab existence. Unable to distinguish between reality and entertainment, many conclude that all Americans are extremely rich and live and behave like these fictional, often extreme sitcom characters.

I remember an incident that took place forty-five years ago when I was growing up in South Africa. My best friend in primary school, with whom I've maintained contact ever since, emigrated from Scotland about the same time my family came from the United States. Although television was not introduced in South Africa until the '70s, he had seen his share of John Wayne and classic Westerns at the local movie theater. One day after coming home from the movies, he asked me in all sincerity, "So Mark, when your dad lived in America, was he a cowboy or a crook?"

A BULL IN THE JUNGLE

Fast-forward thirty-five years to the era when the Chicago Bulls were in their prime and Michael Jordan was an iconic superstar. I am in Indonesia, in the most remote village I have ever visited. Indonesia is as wide as the United States, comprising 17,000 islands and boasting the fourth-largest population in the world. I have crossed the dateline, losing a day on my long flight from Chicago to Jakarta. From Jakarta

I've taken a three-hour flight west to Bengkulu, a two-hour car ride to the small town of Agar Makmur, and finally an hour-long ride on the back of a motor scooter down winding dirt footpaths. No roads lead from the town to the farms of the microloan recipients I'm going to visit. These residents are first-generation inhabitants of an area that only a couple decades earlier had been dense, uninhabited virgin jungle.

After my first night on the island, I awake to the sound of not only roosters but other birds whose angelic songs ring through the stillness, songs I have never heard before. Dawn is breaking when I decide to take a stroll down the dirt road that leads out of the little village. I come across two boys who look to be about eight years old. They recognize me as a foreigner and eagerly try out the few English words they have no doubt been learning in school.

"Good morning, sir," one of them calls out boldly as I approach.

"Good morning, boys," I reply without breaking my stride.

Proud to be understood, the lad who offered the original friendly greeting follows with the standard "How are you?"

"Fine, thank you," I respond as I smile and make eye contact without slowing down.

Apparently he has exhausted his English repertoire and repeats the formal salutation, "Good morning, sir."

"Good morning, boys," I reply again, this time over my shoulder as I pass, leaving them standing on the side of the path.

"How are you?" the other one calls out, also wanting to participate in this engaging conversation.

"Fine, thank you," I repeat as I keep walking.

And so it goes, each boy practicing what he had been taught in school. I keep walking, never to see them again, though I can hear them for a long distance. Other than the birds and the boys, all else is silent. I continue my walk as the boys continue their greeting. For about ten minutes I can still hear them faintly across the valley as their simple English words reverberate through the still, tropical forest and pristine air, "Good morning, sir. How are you?" I don't know how much longer they persist, but eventually, even in the quietness of the jungle, their voices are no longer discernable.

I extend my journey another fifteen minutes or so before making an about-face and heading home. After retracing my steps for a while, I come upon another boy, this one just a little older than the first two. Perhaps feeling a bit guilty that I'd made so little effort to be friendly earlier, this time I stop and initiate the greeting. "Good morning."

This boy is somewhat more reserved than the others. (Or perhaps it only appears that way because he is alone, without the support of a friend.) Nonetheless, he seems pleased that I have paused and echoes their salutation, "Good morning, sir. How are you?"

"Fine, thank you," I answer, thinking to myself that these boys must all go to the same school. This one is a grade or two ahead of the others; he has a follow-up response memorized and ready to be used. "Where do you live?"

"Chicago," I blurt out before thinking. I probably should have just stuck with America. How would this little fellow, in this remote village nestled deep in the jungle, know Chicago from Timbuktu?

I couldn't have been more mistaken. Without a moment's hesitation, with wide eyes and unabashed glee, he erupts, "Michael Jordan!"

I look at him, shaking my head in disbelief. "Michael Jordan," I reply, now nodding in agreement, not sure which of us is more dumbfounded. I walk back to the place I am staying, trying to figure out what just happened. There I was in the most desolate place I have ever visited, hundreds of miles from what most would consider civilization, in a place that twenty years ago was uninhabited, and a child no more than ten years old knows the line-up of my hometown basketball team.

How does this happen?

In his analysis of world poverty, author Prahalad provides voluminous statistics and examples of just how well connected and networked the world's poorest people are, those who make up what he calls "the bottom of the pyramid" (BOP). He points out that in addition to televisions, wireless phones are rapidly becoming the norm among them. In Africa, an estimated nine in ten phones are mobile phones, and more than sixty-five percent of people are connected through a mobile device. *Time* magazine announced on May 31, 2010, that mobile phone use in developing countries had more than doubled since 2005. And in 2012, *The Economist* reported that China was reaching its billionth mobile phone subscription.

According to Prahalad:

The spread of wireless devices, PC kiosks, and personal digital assistants (PDAs) at the BOP has surprised many a manager and researcher. For example, ITC, an Indian conglomerate, decided to connect Indian farmers with PCs in their villages. The ITC . . . allowed the farmers to check prices not only in the local auction houses (called *mandi*s), but also prices of soybean futures at the Chicago Board of Trade. [The] network allowed the farmers access to information that allowed them to make decisions about how much to sell and when, thus improving their margins. Similarly, women entrepreneurs in southern India, given a PC kiosk in their villages, have learned to videoconference among themselves, across villages on all kinds of issues, from the cost of loans from various banks to the lives of their grandchildren in the United States. Chat rooms are full of activity that none of us could have imagined. Most interestingly, in Kerala, India, fishermen in traditional fishing boats, after a day of productive work, sell their catch to the highest bidders, using their cell phones to contact multiple possible landing sites along the Kerala coast. The simple boats, called catamarans, have not changed, but the entire process of pricing the catch and knowing how to sell based on reliable information has totally changed lives at the BOP.

GLOBAL WINDOW SHOPPING

Increasingly the poor watch those of us who live on the "other side of the tracks" in our global village. What I own or how I behave is no longer only my business. It is known by others across the globe. These working poor are smart enough to understand what they see. They know that my actions and consumption affect what they own and how they live. They see the rich getting richer at their expense, richer because of their cheaper labor and less expensive manufactured goods. Those who are educated watch the West deplete an inordinate proportion of the world's natural resources. They see us pollute the environment, deplete the ozone, and negatively affect the climate of the planet.

Their planet.

As the rich lead the charge of globalization, millions of poor people look on, realizing the majority of them are not reaping many benefits promised by the wealthier nations. Two years before terrorists struck the World Trade Center, J. Orstrom Moller warned of a major clash between rich and poor in a Global Policy Forum article, "The Growing Challenge to Internationalism." "Around the world, ordinary people—not the political and intellectual elite—are asking whether the international system really delivers the goods. Are we better off participating in that system or would it be preferable to turn around and begin a nationalistic policy?"

Moller went on to describe the concerns of the poor when large multinational companies begin doing business in their countries. "On one page of the business paper there may be a story about the CEO of a supranational enterprise earning $25 million. On the next page there may be a story about the same enterprise laying off eight thousand workers. For many people this is unacceptable. It strengthens their belief that the elite takes care of itself and is totally unconcerned by what happens to the rest of the people. Anger is provoked further when, after thousands of layoffs, the plant is moved to another nation."

The parents of the boy in Indonesia who knew that Michael Jordan played for the Chicago Bulls pick up these same news stories on television. They know that the American clothing and footwear manufacturer closed operations in their country and moved them to, say, Vietnam to save a few cents per hour on labor costs.

Equally important, this heightened awareness on the part of the poor is happening at the same time the gap is escalating between the richest and poorest members of the global community. We need consider only a smattering of statistics to recognize just how wide that gap has become:

- While over one billion people live in extreme poverty (less than $1.25 per day), forty individuals collectively own nearly $1 trillion.

- In 2012, the wealth of the three richest people in the world exceeded the combined gross domestic product of the poorest forty-eight nations.

- By the beginning of this century the wealth of the world's 475 billionaires was greater than the combined income of half of humanity.

According to the *CIA World Factbook*, the GDP per capita income of the world in 2011 was $12,000, meaning that the average income of all adults in the world was approximately $1,000 a month. But consider the discrepancies between developed and developing countries: for Europe, per capita income was $38,400 in Germany, $20,600 in Poland, and $7,800 in Albania. In Asia, the average person in the Philippines earned $4,100, in Indonesia $4,700, and in India $3,700. In Central America, Honduras came in at $4,400, Nicaragua at $3,200, and Haiti at $1,300. Ghana in Africa was $3,100, Rwanda $1,400, and the Democratic Republic of the Congo a shocking $400. Contrast all of these examples with the U.S., where our per capita income was $49,000.

This widening gap between the haves and have-nots is not a matter of statistics or ratios or personal net worth. It affects real people and their families, permeating every element that makes for a healthy individual and society: education, healthcare, nutrition, clean water, and more. In parts of the world, millions die from mosquito-transmitted malaria, while elsewhere small fortunes are spent (and made) on cosmetic surgery.

Zbigniew Brzezinski, national security advisor under President Jimmy Carter, highlighted the severity of this contrast and its ripple effect on people's well-being: "There is a growing disparity in the human condition, not only in wealth, but in the development of science and technology. This in turn leads to a vast disparity in the quality of life— millions are dying of AIDS in Africa, while therapeutic cloning is taking place in the United States."

WHO BENEFITS FROM OUR GENEROSITY?

The good news is that Americans as a whole are pretty generous people. We volunteer great amounts of time, energy, and money to people in need and deserving causes. For example, within two weeks following Hurricane Katrina, Americans donated more than $1 billion to help the people of New Orleans.

Each year the AAFRC Trust for Philanthropy conducts research on the philanthropic behavior of citizens of our country using information from the Internal Revenue Service. The analysis is issued in an annual publication titled "Giving USA." The report does not monitor federal grants or other governmental support provided by tax dollars, but measures voluntary giving from the private sector. Information includes, among other things, where the donations come from (individuals, foundations, bequests, and corporations) and where they go (religion, education, health, human services, arts, environment, and international affairs).

The most recent analysis is from 2011. During that year, Americans voluntarily contributed a colossal $298.42 billion to charity. That is a lot of money freely given away. An estimated 88 percent of that was donated by individuals, either while they were living or upon their death through bequests. The balance came from foundations and corporations.

As impressive as our individual generosity may be, the disheartening side of the equation is what we give those dollars to and where the money goes. Of the $298 billion in private donations given to charity, less than $24 billion is designated to international aid. That means about 92 percent of all money voluntarily donated by individual Americans goes directly back into America to benefit us and our society—back to the nation whose gross domestic product already accounts for 20 percent of the GDP of the entire world. Back to where the average family is making more than four times the average of everyone in the entire world, and more than one hundred times the income of the average family in the poorest countries.

The money donated in 2005 during the two weeks after Katrina to help disaster survivors in Louisiana was 250 percent greater than the amount given in the same period following the tsunami in the Indian Ocean one year previous. The devastation in New Orleans, though horrific, paled in comparison to the calamity in Asia and Africa. Eighteen hundred Americans lost their lives during one of our nation's worst natural disasters, while 150 times as many people were killed by the Indian Ocean catastrophe.

Highlighting the relatively small amount of donations that are channeled to international needs is not intended to minimize the need and pain in our country. Nor is it to say that the poor in the developing world gain nothing from some of our other contributions. For instance, money given for medical research obviously has the potential of serving all. Having said that, some diseases that affect many in poorer nations are not found in the West and so receive minimal attention. There simply is not the market incentive to drive the private-sector research to find cures or treatment for diseases that are prevalent only in poor countries, where citizens have no health insurance and are less able to purchase the medicines.

Further, some diseases for which medicines do exist continue to destroy lives because the affected people are too poor to pay for the drugs. In 2010 there were 216 million cases of malaria worldwide and an estimated 655,000 deaths, mostly among children in Africa. Malaria is preventable and treatable, but the low-cost tools and medications remain out of economic reach for Africa's poor.

In addition to money given for medical research, some of the money given to religious organizations filters through churches and synagogues to international causes. But only a small percentage of the money given to churches and religious organizations makes it overseas, and those funds are frequently used for religious endeavors rather than for the physical needs of the poor.

Similarly, some of the funds given to educational and environmental causes help everyone living on this planet. But the point stands: we continue to add huge sums to the endowments of our wealthiest universities, and we finance museums and other American institutions for our own edification, while only a token amount of the donations made by this wealthiest of nations helps those living in the poorest countries. Unconscionably, we as Americans designate less than 8 percent of our charitable donations to that half of humanity living on approximately $2 a day—and the poor know it. As Jeffrey Sachs, in his renowned book *The End of Poverty*, succinctly points out, "Spin as we might in the United States about our generosity, the poor countries are fully aware of what we are *not* doing."

Lest these figures become a haze of overwhelming and impersonal statistics, let me distill the situation in our global village to three vital trends.

Trend one: Awareness by the poor is escalating through proliferation of television and international communications.

Trend two: The gap between the richest and the poorest inhabitants of our planet is not only wide, but widening.

Trend three: People with the greatest amount of surplus resources are sharing relatively little with those who have the least.

WHY AWARENESS MATTERS

The convergence of these three trends is creating an untenable condition in our global village today. The working poor have taught me not only that they are very much aware of how we live, but also that they find much of what they know about us to be objectionable. It is not only our perceived materialism and greed that disturbs them. They are offended by some of our other Western values (or lack thereof): disrespect for authority and the elderly, placing a high priority on fashion and external beauty, promiscuity and the erosion of family, abuse of global natural resources, and our unilateral political clout.

I realize that watching "30 Rock" doesn't provide an accurate picture of American life. I also acknowledge that the poor are frequently manipulated by their own political and religious leaders who exploit them for their own agendas. My point here is to underscore a lesson from the working poor that we all need to understand. They are aware of what is going on in the rest of the world, and this awareness has the potential for dire consequences. To put it another way: what if the tables were turned and *you* struggled to feed your family in a world you perceived too full of unjust hurdles set up by powers both at home and, even worse, from far away?

When half of the world's population is barely able to feed itself while the other half indulges and is doing relatively little to change the imbalance, and when the poorest faction of the global community is aware of both these realities, the stage is dangerously set for the poor to lash out against those who consume and control the world's resources. As certain conditions enable a spark to create an explosion, so awareness converts economic disparity into volatility. Extreme poverty does not cause terrorism any more than oxygen creates combustion, but there is no escaping the reality that hopelessness fueled by awareness makes for a fertile breeding ground of unrest and, ultimately, violence. With the epoch of awareness, the pin has been pulled from poverty's grenade.

A few days after the terrorist attacks of September 11, 2001, a meeting took place among leaders of several international nongovernmental organizations, along with the editor-at-large of *Time* magazine and the author of *The American Century*. Their discussion was summarized in the article "Terrorism and the New U.S. Foreign Policy: Views from Abroad," and made available by the Council on Foreign Relations. At that early gathering, "It was generally agreed that if the roots of terrorism are to be addressed, the issue of economic disparity must be addressed."

A few weeks later the Permanent Observer of the Holy See to the United Nations told the First Committee (Disarmament and International Security), "If the international community continues on its current course—more arms and more poverty—the result would be human disasters even greater than those endured on September 11." Convinced that poverty was a significant factor behind the terrorist attacks, he elaborated this caution during the Committee's general debate, "A disservice would be done to those who died in the September tragedy if the world failed to search out the causes. Global economic disparity was fundamentally incompatible with global security; and poverty, along with other forms of marginalization that engulfed the lives of so many people, was a breeding ground for terrorists."

The extent of the correlation between poverty and terrorism continues to be debated. Yet it is widely accepted that when people are desperately poor, they are more easily manipulated. Not long after the September 11 terrorist attacks, President Bush addressed the Inter-American Development Bank stating, "Poverty doesn't cause terrorism. Being poor doesn't make you a murderer. Most of the plotters of September 11th were raised in comfort. Yet persistent poverty and oppression can lead to hopelessness and despair. And when governments fail to meet the most basic needs of their people, these failed states can become havens for terror."

General George C. Marshall offered a warning in 1947 when outlining his plan to help the defeated nations of Europe after World War II. He recognized that many innocent lives had been lost and that without economic security there could be "no political stability and no assured peace." In making his recommendations, he declared that American policy was "directed not against any other country or doctrine but against hunger, poverty, desperation, and chaos."

Fifty-five years later, World Bank president James Wolfensohn acknowledged that world stability remains in jeopardy as long as this economic gap persists. He readily admitted that our self-interest is intertwined with the economic growth of developing countries. Until the poor have jobs and an equal shot at participating in the world's economy, we will not have a just and stable global village. In 2002 at China's Peking University he proposed practical strategies to narrow the gap, such as "treating the poor not as objects of charity, but as assets on which we can build a better and safer world." His recommendation included "microcredit, where the poor are at the center of the solution, not at the end of a handout."

In March 2004 these two international leaders were quoted by Lieutenant General Claudia J. Kennedy, who retired from the U.S. Army in 2000 after becoming the first woman to reach the rank of three-star general. She had just returned from a trip to the Dominican Republic during which she had inspected a microfinance program and visited some of the borrowers.

Referring to General Marshall's post-World War II observation, General Kennedy said, "Today the challenge is at least as great— probably greater. With billions of people suffering economic deprivation, the relationship between economic instability and political instability leading to terrorism is ominous. For this and humanitarian reasons, [we have] called for a global version of the Marshall Plan to confront and eradicate chronic poverty worldwide . . . absolutely convinced that poverty is a breeding ground of enormous social turmoil, and that this turmoil often results in civil unrest with the potential for worldwide terrorism."

Like James Wolfensohn, General Kennedy was optimistic that solutions to poverty are on the horizon, and illustrated her hope for the audience with an anecdote from her trip. "When I was in the Dominican Republic earlier this week, we met a woman named Catalina, who operated the tiniest little cafeteria you can imagine. When we were talking to her, her face and her posture showed me that she had been absolutely overwhelmed by the insecurity of her life. But she had put her two daughters through school. I saw them in the background, and they were standing up straight. They were proud and self-confident.

Insecurity had definitely been part of their life, but it had not overwhelmed them. The cycle of despair and insecurity had already been broken."

General Kennedy's statement reinforced what I have witnessed all over the world: families are transformed when people work. The income from their jobs is only one of an array of blessings that follow. When chronically impoverished people are freed from the bondage of poverty, all kinds of wonderful things begin to happen. When the poor, instead of standing in line waiting for a handout, are equipped to take initiative and get a hand up, they unleash a power so strong that even a three-star general of the world's most powerful army takes note. Every time a poor mother receives credit so she can work and feed her children, the whole world becomes a better place.

BLISSFUL IGNORANCE IS DAMAGING BLINDNESS

Humanity has a track record of enduring unjust scenarios and allowing atrocities to flourish for years until eventually evil is seen for what it is. God-fearing people wore blinders during the build-up of the Third Reich and the subsequent slaughter of six million Jews. In the United States, many were unable or unwilling to see their bias toward slavery until after it was abolished. When we lived in South Africa, my family constantly heard our white friends rationalize the injustice of apartheid, unable to see wrong in what they were doing and unwilling to recognize rampant exploitation. Knowing this propensity, I must force myself to stand back and look objectively at my position in the world, lest I continue in "blissful" ignorance.

As I write this sentence, I am wearing brand-name sneakers that cost $100, mindful that the people who made them likely earn about twenty cents an hour. How much more would I willingly pay if I could be assured that the person who assembled my clothing received a fair wage? What is fair? Why do I wear brand-name clothes anyway? What's the *real* reason? Why do I have so many pairs of slacks hanging in my closet (six of them khaki, two of them never worn)?

These simple yet perplexing questions remain unresolved. Karl Marx would tell me to give all but a few outfits to the poor or, more accurately, have my government enforce the redistribution. We know how poorly that works. We also know how welfare programs in our own country can create intergenerational dependency and destroy initiative. Guilt about my possessions and good fortune accomplishes no more than apathy.

So how do you and I respond to *our* awareness? While the poor have taught me that they know how *we* live, the reverse is also true. We can no longer plead ignorance, because technology works both ways. We know how *they* live. We often see the poor on the news and increasingly hear about their living conditions. Our churches send mission teams to build shelters and they bring back stories and pictures that break our hearts. But broken hearts aren't enough. Awareness must lead to action.

What I find so exciting and promising is that it doesn't take much for us to help transform hopelessness into success. Today, most of us will use our credit cards to buy something we don't really need, the cost of which could provide a month's worth of emergency food relief for a family in Kenya or set someone up in Colombia with a small loan to start a business. I don't say this to make anyone feel guilty, but to expand our collective vision.

In the Anglican tradition there is a wonderful liturgical refrain that is repeated by the congregation throughout particular prayers. Speaking on behalf of the group, the priest recites a brief commitment to God regarding a specific action. At the end of each statement, the group responds in unison, "I will, with God's help." This acknowledges that God often calls us to behavior that is counterintuitive, and that we need extra grace and strength to swim against the stream of our culture and society.

As I reflect on the poverty in the world and the undeserved place of privilege that I enjoy, I resolve afresh to let my own awareness prompt me to action. Will you join me?

Together, let us respond: "I will, with God's help."

11

FINAL LESSONS

God loves the poor, and so should we.

I have known John and Jacque for twenty years. You'd never know it by talking with these dear friends, or by visiting their modest home, but they have been blessed with great financial success. John started a small furniture business, and over the course of thirty years amassed a sizable estate. About the time most successful entrepreneurs would reinvest in another venture or grow their net worth for retirement, John placed everything in a trust to empower the poor. He spent the next five years liquidating his business so he could support organizations working in the developing world. I still have the original, deeply moving letter he wrote to me explaining why he had made this radical choice. With his permission, I'm extracting just a few lines from it describing his gratitude to God, his desires for his adult children, his joy in being able to give, how he came to his decision, and his vision to equip those in need to better their lives.

Dear Mark,

You will understand the deep gratitude to God for the gift of life, and the great joy and excitement that we feel as we move into this next phase of our lives together. We have signed the papers that establish the family foundation—"To provide opportunities worldwide for people living in chronic poverty to transform their lives and lift themselves out of poverty."

I didn't know at the time what would come of John's commitment, but when I had my unexpected encounter with God in that hotel room in India (the one I described in chapter seven), of all the names mentioned in my prayer, John and Jacque stood out. I felt a special affection for them. Shortly after returning home, I had a message from John on my answering machine. Recalling my prayer, I was eager to see what God might be arranging. I called him right away. The purpose of John's call was to inform me that he wanted to make a donation of $100,000 to create more jobs for poor people in the developing world. (Over the next ten years that gift provided employment for about 10,000 people.)

That was the beginning. Since then, John and Jacque have given away tens of millions of dollars in support of microfinance. I will always cherish the long walks we have taken together, sharing our journeys and passion for the poor. He has become a model for me, not only in terms of sharing my own personal resources, but doing so with joy and abandon. Not many are so cheerful about their giving, so thoughtful and strategic, so free.

Interestingly, John does not call himself a Christian. He professes instead to be a follower of Jesus of Nazareth. Semantics? Perhaps, but for John, religious labels just get in the way, meaning different things to different people. Some feel the "Christian" label has been so used and abused that it has lost its true meaning. What's important to John is trying to live as Jesus did, particularly when it comes to responding to those in need. Many years ago, John studied ancient Greek so he could read the New Testament in its original language and better understand and follow Jesus' teaching. John's example taught me that although there may be a lot of confusion about what it means to be a Christian, when you focus on Jesus—what he taught and how he lived—you cannot escape the fact that Jesus had a special place in his heart for those living in poverty.

Jesus was born into poverty. Tradition suggests that his parents' only transportation was a donkey. They had neither clout nor money to finesse their way into a hotel or secure a bed of any kind, despite his mother, Mary, being pregnant. After his birth, kings and astronomers from distant lands arrived. They had been beckoned by an unusual star in the heavens. For many miles and many days they followed this star as it moved slowly across the night sky, visible only to those who had eyes to see and a will to pursue. It led them to a small village named Bethlehem. The star came to rest, mysteriously beaming its light over the place where a poor but holy baby had been born. There they showered the destitute family with extravagant gifts they had brought on their camels: gold, frankincense, and myrrh.

In this pivotal scene of God's cosmic drama, the poor and the rich meet. Before God created the heavens and the earth, he staged this momentous encounter. It was no more an accident that his Son was born among the "have-nots" than that the star directed the "haves" to him. God could have placed Jesus in a family of wealth. He could have orchestrated the politics of the day so that Jesus traveled to the kings. Instead, God constructed a scenario where his holy Child was born in a lowly stable. Then he called the wealthy to come to him with their gifts. All this and much more are part of his eternal plan for humanity.

As an adult, Jesus chose to remain poor despite his unequaled following. One of his devotees said to him, "Teacher, I will follow you wherever you go," to which Jesus replied, "Foxes have holes and birds of the air have nests, but the Son of Man has no place to lay his head" (Matthew 8:20). Jesus did not have a house or closets full of clothing. He lived simply, as did his closest friends, and he instructed his followers to do the same.

When Jesus died, he was so poor his family could not afford a proper burial. A rich man came to him and contributed a tomb where he could be laid. Being born without a bed, living without a house, and dying without a tomb, Jesus was indeed poor from start to finish—not by coincidence, but by divine design. From his poverty he teaches us many rich lessons.

Jesus directed some of his harshest teachings and warnings at the wealthy. Someone once quipped, "God must love the poor very much. Just look how many he made." Intended as a humorous statement, it nonetheless points to a greater truth: God must love the poor very much. Just look how much he had to *say* about them—more than on almost any other topic—and how much he did *for* and *with* them.

If God loves the marginalized with such deep affection, it would follow that we who profess faith in God should view them with equally high esteem. They are not only a statistic or a topic of discussion and debate; they are unique individuals, made in God's image with immeasurable worth. Many are extravagantly gifted, energetic, and enterprising people, eager to provide for their families and live fulfilling lives. When we see them as God sees them, they radiate beauty and dignity that deserve our respect.

Having worked for more than two decades with people in the developing world, I have also learned that for the most part, they are not responsible for their poverty. While there are many complex reasons that help explain why so many people live on $1.25 a day, the greatest factor determining their situation is latitude and longitude. If you are born in North America or Western Europe, you have almost no chance of being on the world's bottom rung. The odds are reversed for those born in parts of Asia and most of sub-Saharan Africa. You have no control over where you were born. This becomes agonizingly clear when you stand next to someone roughly your own age and gender in the developing world. When you ride a rickshaw in India. When you gaze at Victoria Falls after spending the day with Esther in Zimbabwe. Or when you refuse to buy potholders from a little girl in Guatemala.

When you fully grasp the meaning of this important lesson—that the poor are not living in slums by choice or because they're unwilling to do what is necessary to escape—it changes your attitude about them. The poor have immense capabilities, but unjust conditions make it virtually impossible for millions to escape generational poverty. Without creative intervention, we cannot expect them to break the cycle into which they were born.

We cannot accept the misconception that eradicating poverty is a hopeless cause. Yes, there will always be some who have less than others. But the kind of extreme poverty endured by more than a billion people can be erased. There are encouraging signs that this is finally being recognized. Just think of the "impossibilities" we have accomplished in recent history. During the twentieth century the heinous polio pandemic killed and crippled millions of people, particularly children. Yes, there were those who thought we could never eradicate this dreaded disease. But thanks to the vision and dedication of many good people, especially the work of Rotary International, polio was defeated. A few brave individuals with great vision accomplished in one generation what most of the world considered impossible.

Similarly, there was a time when apartheid in South Africa and slavery in America were considered the status quo. Many good people thought it was wrong to treat people so unjustly, but accepted it as "just the way things were." Today, both slavery in America and apartheid in South Africa are gone because good people believed they *could* change the worlds they lived in, and did.

In just one generation we went from horses and buggies to automobiles to propeller-driven airplanes to sending people to the moon. If someone had told my grandfather that a man would walk on the moon, he would have laughed at the impossibility of it. If someone had told me when I was in college that one day I would be writing a book on a computer that I carry with me all over the world, I would have laughed. If I had been told that I would be in a remote village in China talking on a portable telephone with my son in New York City, I would have laughed even louder. Today that son writes and records music in his apartment in Queens, his friend mixes the songs in his studio in Los Angeles, and I listen to them while driving down the highway in Chicago—all done in cyberspace with no travel, no postage, and no record album.

Eradicating poverty in the twenty-first century is another of those "impossibilities." The only reason a goal like this is impossible is that we *choose* to make it impossible. We have the resources to get the job done. The money some of us waste in a single day would feed a family of four in Sudan for a week. If we directed our loose change to ventures that train and empower people to feed themselves, poverty could become the horse and buggy of our century—only a distant memory. Each of us has a role to play, a choice to make. Poverty will not be wiped out by politics or governments, though they clearly have great potential to either worsen poverty or find solutions. It's individuals like you and me who will make it happen, first by deciding that the battle can be won, and second, by choosing to join the fight. Yes, there will always be pockets of society that resist fixing until certain systemic changes are made or until corrupt political leaders are replaced. But we don't have to wait for those areas to be resolved before addressing the whole. And you don't have to be wealthy or famous or powerful to make a difference. You just have to care and be willing to act, to be the hands and feet of a loving God.

WHAT CAN *I* DO?

Sometimes when I talk to people, it's clear they have a tender spot in their hearts and want to do something about this injustice. But other than putting some money in an envelope or promising to pray for the poor—both of which are important—they express an understandable sense of futility: "It's just such an overwhelming problem. I really can't make much of a difference."

If that's how *you* feel, I'd like to challenge your thinking. First, I think we underestimate the power of prayer. Somehow, in ways I don't understand, God does listen and respond. Prayer is a powerful resource capable of moving mountains, yet we tend to treat it as if it is the least effective weapon in our arsenal. Money, legislation, regime change—those are the big guns. I'm just an ordinary working stiff, you might think—all I can do is pray. If everyone who loves God would commit to pray, I honestly believe that alone would eradicate poverty. If reading this book motivates you to set aside regular time to pray for an end to poverty, the writing has been worth it. As people of faith, prayer is our most powerful resource.

God gave us the gift of faith so we might put it to work. St. James, who called himself a servant of Jesus, wrote, "Faith by itself, if it is not accompanied by action, is dead" (James 2:17). In addition to praying, you can do many things that will move us closer to unpoverty. One size does not fit all when it comes to our practical response, any more than a simple formula can determine how much is enough when giving to charity. The following list is not exhaustive, but might trigger some additional ideas of your own. You will see that turning your faith into action will not only be relatively easy; it will be fun:

• *Pay attention.* Learn more about poor people in your community and around the world. If you are part of a church or other religious group, find out what it is doing to help the poor. Develop an ear for the poor as you go about your day.

• *Expand your boundaries.* Despite our shrinking planet, most of the news we receive is about ourselves. Seek out media outlets that report on conditions around the world. One excellent source is the BBC World Service, which is available through many NPR affiliates. Also, use the power and reach of the Internet to learn more about your global neighbors.

• *Travel.* Instead of visiting Paris, go to Peru or Panama. Try to get off the tourist-beaten path and visit people where they live and work. You don't have to gawk as if watching animals at the zoo. There are respectful and honoring ways to observe. One year I took a couple and their grandkids to Colombia. Fred had been a generous supporter for two decades and he wanted to pass on his passion and values to his grandkids. I think he's succeeding. At the end of the trip, referring to the families we'd met, ten-year-old Kevin said, "They have so little and they're so grateful." He gets it.

• *Become an informal advocate.* Use what you have learned in this book and other sources to speak up for the poor within your circles of influence: your family and friends, neighbors, colleagues at work. If someone makes a disparaging comment about the poor, be the one who defends their honor and dignity. Tell them about Esther or Setiawan or Father Ben.

• *Help a new arrival.* In nearly every city in the United States, you will find small communities of recent immigrants and social service agencies who rely on volunteers to help these immigrants with everything from learning conversational English to figuring out how to use public transportation to finding employment. Not only will you help people avoid falling into poverty, it's a great way to learn about another country and culture.

• *Write a letter.* Although poverty won't be eradicated by government action, it never hurts to have a little help in high places. Write your members of Congress and ask them what they are doing to reduce poverty around the world. Encourage them to stand up for the rights of the poor at home and abroad. When they vote for laws that assist poor people, write them again to thank them. Many humanitarian organizations offer support that makes advocacy easy. For example, visit www.worldvision.org and click on the Get Involved tab.

• *Adopt a developing nation.* Select a country plagued by poverty and learn everything you can about it. This is a great way for grandparents or parents of younger children to help their kids become global citizens. Using the Internet and other resources, help them recognize the country's flag, learn about the culture and religion, and understand what people do there to earn a living. Prepare a meal that would be typical for a family in that country. Consider sponsoring a child from that country through World Vision. For an unforgettable family vacation, save up for a few years and visit your adopted country.

• *Examine your lifestyle.* I rushed into a local men's clothing store recently because they had advertised a going-out-of-business sale. Good stewardship, right? Save money on clothes so I can give to the poor. By the time I left the store, I had bought more than I normally would have, and a whole lot more than I needed. Right then, I resolved to be more diligent about not spending on things I don't really need. If you look closely at how you spend money, you, too, will likely find ways to adjust your lifestyle so you can be more charitable.

• *Join an international trip.* The next time your church sponsors a trip to El Salvador to build a health clinic, sign up. International trips aren't just about what you'll contribute. You'll gain far more than you give, but that's okay. Just go with that understanding. Most people who go on these trips call it life-changing. What usually changes is your perception of the poor as you witness their ability to be joyful despite their circumstances and learn how much you have in common. Then come home and be their voice.

• *Partner with professionals.* In the afterword I describe my recent trip to the Horn of Africa with World Vision and provide information about how you can partner with them to help lay a foundation for a better future for some of the world's most vulnerable people. In addition to microfinance, World Vision invests in a wide range of other community development efforts, working alongside local people to provide clean water, healthcare, education, business and agricultural training, and more. Whatever your area of interest, you will find an outlet to serve and give—either through this organization or one of the many other reputable international development organizations working to end extreme poverty.

• *Plan for your second half.* As you approach your fifties, you may be in a position to leave your current job for one that is more rewarding in terms of meaning and significance. You may be financially independent, or your company may offer you a buyout for early retirement. This is a great opportunity to align your skills and knowledge with your passion for the poor. Learn more about this in the book *Halftime* by Bob Buford.

• *Listen to the UnPoverty soundtrack.* My son, Joshua, is writing music to accompany this book. There will be one song for each chapter, which you can sample on my website, www.unpoverty.org. If you've enjoyed the stories, you'll love his songs. That's not just a proud father speaking, although I admit I am one. He has chosen to join the unpoverty revolution, and, as I am doing with this book, is donating all proceeds to charity.

YOU DID IT FOR ME

When Mother Teresa was asked why she gave so much of herself to the poorest of the poor, she answered, "Each one of them is Jesus in disguise." In this she was reflecting Jesus' own teaching: "Whatever you did for one of the least of these brothers of mine, you did for me" (Matthew 25:40). There are a lot of reasons why we need to act, but for me, this is the greatest motivator. The poor are a proxy for Jesus. When I serve them, I serve him. When I am a voice for those whose voices are not heard, I am his voice. When I care for them, I come as one of the Magi, carrying gifts to the poor and to the holy Child. We do not all bring the same gifts. We each offer from the abundance with which we have been blessed. I cannot give what I do not have. I offer respect as I begin to put faces on the statistics. I honor poor people as I acknowledge my own poverty and learn from their richness.

The prophet Micah tells us that what God really wants from us is to do justice, love kindness, and walk humbly before him.

We *do justice* when we seek to level the field by providing everyone with opportunities to transform their lives.

We *love kindness* when we make choices that grant them more options and freedom.

We *walk humbly before God* when we do all we can to meet the needs of those he loves so very much, yet trust him for the results.

Thankfully, the earth rests permanently in the capable hands of the One who created it. While we seek to be faithful in the battle against poverty, our loving God is gently embracing the entire world and tenderly repeating, "It's all mine."

In this spirit, then, I invite you to join me along with a growing chorus of voices who are saying "We can do it!" As finite individuals, it might seem like a preposterous goal to try to eliminate extreme poverty, but if all of us take enough of the steps suggested in this chapter, then we'll have done our part. Couple that with the people you've read about in these pages—and the extraordinary contributions they routinely make to provide solutions to injustice and inequality—and together we'll make a quantum leap toward the goal of eradicating extreme poverty in our lifetime. We serve a great God who loves all of his children and offers us the wonderful privilege of becoming his agents of healing and change. That's how God works.

The only hope the poor have for experiencing that change is you. And me. And anyone else who cares enough to join this exciting adventure. I know people audacious enough to believe that, with God, absolutely anything is possible. People who are so grateful for the bounty they enjoy that they have to share it with those who have so little. People who acknowledge that, but for a twist of fate, they could be right there in the slums looking through the garbage for something to eat. They know that when they look into the eyes of a poor person, they are looking into the eyes of Jesus.

Few things in life are as rewarding as knowing that a small choice you made has given someone else a chance for a better life. You can play a major role in putting a smile on the face of a child. It's happening every day, and it would be a shame if you never experienced the powerful joy that comes from standing with the poor, rejoicing with all the ordinary people, taking action to end this affliction. One day extreme poverty will be history. When it is, those born into a world without it will wonder why it took so long.

Thank you for what you will do to shape a world of unpoverty.

AFTERWORD

The purpose of *UnPoverty* is to demonstrate that the poor in the developing world are rich in many indispensible ways, deserving not only our respect but also our partnership.

Most of the stories shared in this book are gleaned from my travels over twenty-two years with Opportunity International, one of the earliest and most innovative microfinance organizations. They do one thing, and they do it extremely well.

Since the initial printing of *UnPoverty*, I have joined World Vision, one of the world's largest and most comprehensive humanitarian organizations. They combine microfinance efforts with a host of other interventions, including water, agriculture, education, and much more to address the full range of needs faced by those living in poverty.

When approached with an end goal of empowerment and self-sufficiency, each of these interventions actively engages the poor in discovering and creating their own solutions, resulting in holistic and sustainable community development.

SECURE THE FUTURE

During a trip to eastern Africa in the summer of 2012, I visited Tanzania, a country where eighty percent of the population depends on agriculture. Drastic climate shifts have had a devastating impact on crop yields in recent years, leaving impoverished farmers in this region in grave need of knowledge and tools to cope with new weather patterns.

In each community we visited, I was able to see firsthand how seemingly small aid efforts can make a profound difference for struggling families. Through an innovative initiative called Secure the

Future, World Vision is equipping smallholder farmers to develop and better use local natural resources. The impact of this work is nothing short of astounding.

In many ways, the individuals I met on this trip live as people did in Bible times: children herd animals; donkeys carry heavy burdens; women draw water from wells; sandaled feet walk along dusty paths. But, after centuries of only peripheral change, one of the most basic forces shaping culture and society—the weather—means that many in this region must think and act in new ways. This change is simultaneously a great threat and a tremendous opportunity: how they, and we, respond will quite literally dictate life or death for millions.

In an isolated Tanzanian community situated along a narrow, red-dirt road lives Yohana Karani, a rice farmer who inherited a three-acre plot of land from his father. His father likewise cultivated this plot before him. In previous generations this land was more productive, but fifteen years of frequent droughts interspersed with destructive floods has greatly weakened its capacity.

Yohana's grandfather and father taught him when to plant based on the expected arrival of the rains. But the climatic regularity they once depended on is gone. The rains now come later, if at all. And some years, they arrive in a deluge that washes away the seeds.

Beginning in the early 2000s, sporadic rain—combined with insufficient irrigation and lack of access to quality seeds and fertilizer—have made it nearly impossible for Yohana and his family to earn a living. Each harvest, his land would yield only twenty-eight bags of rice—and because of the inferior grade, each 110-pound bag would sell for the equivalent of barely $22.

Exacerbating the problem, there were seasons when, at planting time, Yohana had no cash to buy seed and was forced to borrow around $60 from a local moneylender. A few months later he would repay the loan shark with six bags of rice, one for every $10 loan, equaling more than 220 percent interest.

But at the peak of the drought, along with 5,100 other local farmers, Yohana registered for the Secure the Future project, and his family's life began to be transformed.

In the recent past, these subsistence farmers—each cultivating between one and three acres of land—were able to grow only enough to feed their immediate families. Little remained to sell. Participating in the project, Yohana joined a commercial producer group of about twenty-five smallholder farmers, which in turn united with twenty-four similar groups to form a "commercial village." Farmers in neighboring communities followed the same plan.

These farmers benefited from a consortium of four nonprofit organizations. World Vision brokered the alliance and leveraged its extensive footprint and strong relationships through its unique community development model, which employs a holistic approach to help families become self-sustaining. VisionFund Tanzania, a microfinance bank affiliated with World Vision, provided loans to buy liquid organic fertilizer and high-yielding seeds. MicroEnsure, a subsidiary of Opportunity International, provided weather-indexed insurance to mitigate the risks for both farmers and lenders. Farm Concern International, which is networked throughout eastern Africa, trained the farmers to aggregate their production, equipping them to create trading blocs and compete with commercial farms to attract buyers that purchase large quantities of rice in a single transaction. The farmers' favorable prices achieved through this economy of scale, coupled with increased buyer competition, resulted in a remarkable increase in farmer incomes.

In the second of last year's two growing seasons, Yohana harvested sixty-eight bags of rice, 242 percent of what he produced before. And because he's using better seeds and fertilizer, the quality of his crop now equals the standard set for large commercial farmers. No longer is he selling a paltry few bags of rice at a low price. Now that he is part of a trading bloc, he deals with commercial buyers who are interested in larger purchases and willing to pay better prices.

For the first time ever, a large semi-truck—from neighboring Uganda, no less—rumbled into Yohana's community and bought every bag that they and the neighboring commercial villages would sell. Best of all, Yohana received the equivalent of about $56 for each bag of rice—well over twice what his previous crop had garnered.

All told, Yohana's sales in one season increased from $664 to $3,920, resulting in an annual increase that borders on miraculous. In fact, some farmers not participating in the program refused at first to believe it. I was told that one particularly cynical farmer insisted on counting the bags himself!

And the story really only begins there. This success has birthed new hope and confidence in the farmers of Yohana's community, who are already planning for the next phase of improvements. By processing their harvested rice through a machine that sifts out stones, sticks, and chaff, they will be able to demand an even higher price. When we visited, they had already identified the optimum machine, which costs about $10,000.

What was most notable was that they did not ask us to give them the machine or the money to buy it. They had already begun a savings club that they were all adding to regularly. Their only request was that once they'd saved $5,000, we extend them a microloan for the balance. With the higher profits from their improved produce, they will repay that loan in only two seasons.

Beyond the processing machine, the group is also making plans to invest in appropriate storage facilities for their increased yields. Presently, they have no alternative but to sell their crops immediately after the harvest to avoid the risk of damage from weather, thieves, or animals. However, at the close of the season, when supply is up and demand down, prices are at their lowest. When Yohana harvested his rice this past season, he kept ten bags for his family's consumption but immediately sold the balance. Every farmer in his commercial village did the same, selling their crops as soon as they were harvested. Creating facilities to store their crops for a few months would enable them to significantly improve the return on their investment.

As much as I marveled at their dreams for the future, I was equally taken by what this group of farmers had already accomplished. When we met with them, they took turns proudly recounting the project's many benefits for their families. For example, now that his family has a more reliable means of income, Yohana's daughter is now able to attend high school. A child of one of the other farmers is attending college in pursuit of a journalism degree. Several farmers boasted of being able to plaster their houses with concrete—no minor improvement, given that the mud-brick walls gradually erode as a result of the weather.

One farmer bought a bicycle—a "luxury" that transforms lives in communities where many walk for hours every day, often barefoot. Another bought a foot-pedaled sewing machine and established an enterprise that benefits community members who have never entered a shopping mall or even a clothing store. Several farmers bought pigs, and many purchased goats that provide nutritious milk to supplement their family's diet.

These individual accomplishments came as no great surprise, however, as I reflected on the heroic achievement I had just witnessed the previous day. We had visited a region that is now home to the longest manmade river in Tanzania—a hand-dug canal that stretches one hundred miles. Mile after mile, and village by village, the local farmers had been mobilized to meet their own needs and bring water to their fields. The excavation was accomplished over the course of two years through a food-for-work program that compensated the farmers with nutritious food for their families.

Through an impressive array of channels and gates, life-giving water now flows from a natural spring in the mountains to irrigate some eight thousand small farms. To ensure fair access for every farmer, each community has appointed a representative to the council that governs the program and has elected officers to oversee access to the supply. Clearly, one of the central objectives of Secure the Future is being realized—providing a reliable source of water to subsistence farmers formerly dependent on erratic rainfall.

AN INVITATION TO PARTNER WITH THE POOR

The courage, ambition, and resourcefulness of Yohana and his community inspire me to do everything in my power to help people like them fulfill their dreams—and to exhort others to expand this exciting work. These hardworking farmers are not looking for a handout—they're looking for partnership.

It is urgent that we act decisively, strategically, and generously. Those facing the greatest risk from the ongoing shift in weather patterns are those who are already the most vulnerable. If you and I were to face this situation, we would simply pay a little more for the resources we needed.

But communities like Yohana's require drastically different responses, like the ones I witnessed—redirecting a natural water supply, obtaining loans for fertilizer and a more resilient strain of rice, weather-indexed insurance, training and access to new markets.

In my visits to Rwanda and Kenya, I saw other circumstances that required different strategies from the ones employed in Tanzania. But there is a common denominator in every one of these projects: local people are the ones who identify and then prioritize their own needs. Only with their input is a strategy mapped out. After the assessment phase, which can take one to two years, World Vision staff walk alongside community leaders—not giving handouts, but empowering them to create sustainable change that will last long after the organization has moved on to serve another community.

The essential ingredient in the recipe is economic development. Around this cornerstone, every other intervention becomes more effective and lasting. That's why I've committed my life to this work, why I wrote this book, and why I'm inviting you to join me in extending this life-changing opportunity to more deserving people.

Throughout the pages of *UnPoverty* I've posed many questions, some of which remain unresolved in my own mind. Will you join me in continuing to pursue answers, and striving to live in a way that contributes to a more just and stable world?

As part of that journey, I urge you to begin or build on your connection with the poor by giving sacrificially from the resources entrusted to you. If you are not already supporting a charity that empowers hardworking people in the developing world, I encourage you to select one. In the final section of this book, you can read about the comprehensive work of World Vision, the organization I'm now aligned with. There are many others making valuable contributions to eradicate poverty. I'm not lobbying for a particular organization; I'm asking only that you diversify your giving portfolio to include support for those in developing nations who are eager to work and lift their families out of poverty.

It's a telling fact that 92 percent of all charitable donations made by Americans support organizations that benefit our own wealthy nation. Churches and synagogues receive about a third of all charitable dollars.

Universities, human and health services, and domestic social causes also rank high.

These are all worthy and important causes that my wife and I have included in our own charitable giving. Nevertheless, it is unconscionable that only 8 percent of our nation's voluntary contributions are earmarked for the needs of the billions in our world—nearly half of the planet's population—who live on $2 or less a day.

One of the common arguments I hear, especially since the economic downturn in 2008, is that we must address our own country's needs first. The implication (and on occasion, the expressed view) is that our responsibility is to our own nation, and that those living elsewhere should take care of their own problems.

In contrast, Jesus taught that we are to intentionally support those in need regardless of their race or nationality, as illustrated in his well-known parable of the good Samaritan. Because our neighbors, as Jesus defines them, are not always our own countrymen, I leave you with one final story from my most recent trip to Africa. It's a reminder of why I so admire the spirit of the people with whom we work, and why I encourage you to stand in solidarity with them.

THE GIFT OF WATER

Following a three-hour drive over bumpy, dusty, narrow roads, we reached a remote community in arid eastern Kenya, far removed from the nearest source of electricity or running water. Several years earlier, World Vision had drilled a well and installed a solar-powered water pump in this village. For an hour, we stood at the water supply as woman after woman filled containers with water for drinking, cooking, and washing.

As we talked with these women, we learned about their families, their challenges, and how the well had transformed their lives. Gathering water is still an everyday necessity. But on most days, with the sun shining brightly and the solar pump working at full capacity, it now takes as little as thirty minutes.

Prior to the installation of the pump, the women had to lead their donkeys down the hill, across an expansive valley, and up the hill on the other side to the nearest spring. The daily trek took between eight and nine hours. Some days, when the line at the spring was especially long, reaching home before dark was not guaranteed, so the women would spend the night there and return to their families the following morning—perhaps with nursing babies strapped to their backs.

While talking with the women, I couldn't help but think of the potential that the well had created for new microenterprises. Hundreds of hardworking people had suddenly reclaimed eight productive hours each day. Having seen this happen elsewhere, I could envision them engaging in baking, tailoring, carpentry, brickmaking, and a host of other trades that would create capital and economic growth. Improved access to water has transformed their lives, but the opportunity to create enterprises will build their communities.

Those conversations at the well were fresh in my mind the following morning as we visited a nearby primary school, where some of the classes gathered under shady trees because school construction was still in progress. Several large water tanks had been constructed to capture precious rainwater from the classroom roofs. But in this near-desert climate, with no significant rain in two years, the tanks were depleted.

We talked to the dedicated headmaster, who was literally building the school one brick at a time. Two blocks of four classrooms each were currently in use. Another was waiting for a roof, and yet another had walls about two feet high. Like all the homes and buildings in the village, the walls were made from mud bricks baked in the sun.

We asked the headmaster where the bricks came from. His answer was deeply humbling: for years, his students' parents had been donating the freshly baked bricks one or two at a time, generously offering one of their most valuable possessions—that precious commodity they'd had to walk eight hours to gather—to mix with sand and create the mud.

These bricks were their contribution, given from grateful hearts, to the school he was creating for their community. Today, just as they have been freed from their excruciating daily journey for water, their children no longer need to walk several hours to get to class.

Whatever I give to support these heroes—including all the proceeds from this book—pales in comparison to what the families themselves contribute. They are not waiting with open hands to receive charity. Rather, they are contributing sacrificially from their scarcity to address their own needs. They are not merely building walls, or classrooms, or even a school. These families are building a brighter future for their children.

Please join with us, and them, in a mounting revolution to end extreme poverty. Give to help people build their own ladder out of poverty. Give joyfully and lavishly—not out of guilt, but out of gratitude. On behalf of those whose lives can and will be changed, thank you for what you will do to create a world of unpoverty.

I welcome your comments and questions.

Mark Lutz, Director of Global Philanthropy, World Vision
UnPoverty Communications
P.O. Box 3112
Glen Ellyn, IL 60138
mark@unpoverty.org
www.unpoverty.org

World Vision®
Building a better world for children

ABOUT WORLD VISION

World Vision is a Christian humanitarian organization dedicated to working with children, families, and their communities worldwide to reach their full potential by tackling the causes of poverty and injustice. Motivated by our faith in Jesus Christ, World Vision serves alongside the poor and oppressed as a demonstration of God's unconditional love for all people.

Experience | With more than 60 years of experience in working to build a better world for children, World Vision offers hope and assistance to children and families in need in nearly 100 countries—serving everyone, regardless of religion, race, ethnicity, or gender.

Excellence | The quality and effectiveness of our work is affirmed not only by the millions who, in partnership with us, have loosened poverty's grip on their lives, but by the trust of donors, child sponsors, volunteers, advocates, churches, corporations, and government agencies in the United States and around the world.

Efficiency | World Vision has been consistently ranked as a top nonprofit in the area of fiscal responsibility: in the past decade, the percentage of our annual operating expenses going to programs that benefit those in need has fallen between 85 and 89 percent.

WORLD VISION'S APPROACH

Recognizing the complex and interwoven issues that keep families trapped in the cycle of poverty, we have developed a proven, holistic approach to development that centers on partnering with and equipping families and communities to grow physically, socially, and spiritually.

A few of the key areas in which we focus are:

Economic Development | Our microfinance affiliate, VisionFund, has nearly 20 years of experience and a network of microfinance institutions that crosses the globe. Through these institutions, we provide hardworking entrepreneurs with services like small loans to start and grow their businesses and a safe place to deposit their earnings, as well as options like life insurance and access to crop and health insurance to help build their financial resilience.

Water, Sanitation, and Hygiene | Because water is fundamental to life, providing access to clean water and sanitation is a critical humanitarian intervention—and often the first work World Vision undertakes in a community. Our efforts include assistance like drilling and repairing wells, training community members to maintain wells, and building latrines in schools and clinics.

Malaria | Serving in 62 countries affected by malaria, World Vision has prioritized the fight against this deadly disease, which undermines development work and keeps families trapped in the cycle of poverty. Through partnerships with Roll Back Malaria, the Global Fund, and others, we are working to contribute to the Millennium Development Goal of zero malaria deaths.

Child Protection | Millions of children living in poverty face exploitation such as child labor, sex slavery, and early or forced marriage. World Vision embraces a three-fold child protection strategy that includes prevention efforts such as training in parenting skills and economic opportunities for families; protection efforts like temporary shelter, Child-Friendly Spaces, and critical healthcare; and restoration efforts such as life-skills training, support in returning to mainstream education, and reintegration with families where possible.

Christian Witness | World Vision's driving motivation is to demonstrate God's unconditional love through service to those in need. In communities around the world we equip church leaders, integrate biblically based values in our development work, and build bridges with those of other faiths, all with the goal of enabling children to experience fullness of life and the love of God. In countries where expressions of Christian faith are limited, World Vision staff serve as living witnesses through their lives and deeds.

Learn more about World Vision and get involved!

World Vision
P.O. Box 9716
Federal Way, WA 98063-9716
1.888.511.6443
www.worldvision.org